Controversies in Sociology
edited by
Professor T. B. Bottomore and Dr M. J. Mulkay

10
Sociology
and
History

Controversies in Sociology

Sociology
and
History

PETER BURKE

Fellow of Emmanuel College, Cambridge

London
GEORGE ALLEN & UNWIN
Boston   Sydney

First published in 1980

This book is copyright under the Berne Convention. All rights
are reserved. Apart from any fair dealing for the purpose of
private study, research, criticism or review, as permitted under
the Copyright Act, 1956, no part of this publication may be
reproduced, stored in a retrieval system, or transmitted, in any
form or by any means, electronic, electrical, chemical,
mechanical, optical, photocopying, recording or otherwise,
without the prior permission of the copyright owner. Enquiries
should be sent to the publishers at the undermentioned address:

GEORGE ALLEN & UNWIN LTD
40 Museum Street, London WC1A 1LU

© Peter Burke 1980

British Library Cataloguing in Publication Data

Burke, Peter, *b. 1937*
Sociology and history – (Controversies in
Sociology; no. 10).
1. Sociology   2. History
I. Title   II. Series
301   HM36   80-40105

ISBN 0-04-301114-4
ISBN 0-04-301115-2 Pbk

Typeset in 11 on 12 point Times by Red Lion Setters, London
and printed in Great Britain
by Billing and Sons Ltd, London, Guildford & Worcester

By the same author

THE RENAISSANCE SENSE OF THE PAST
  (Edward Arnold, 1969)
CULTURE AND SOCIETY IN RENAISSANCE ITALY
  (Batsford, 1972)
VENICE AND AMSTERDAM (Temple Smith, 1974)
POPULAR CULTURE IN EARLY MODERN EUROPE
  (Temple Smith, 1978)

Contents

for Zev

Preface

This is a two-headed book, facing in two directions at once, because it is written for, as well as about, both sociologists and historians. For this reason I have tried to take very little for granted. The reader should be warned about the author's professional bias. I was trained as a historian and still practise as one, concentrating on the cultural and social history of Europe in the sixteenth and seventeenth centuries. It was the attempt to write social history which led to my involvement with sociology and also with social anthropology, a discipline which plays a more important role in this essay than the title suggests. I owe a considerable debt to sociologists and social anthropologists at the University of Sussex and elsewhere who have helped me understand something of what they do and why they do it, and also to fellow historians who have moved in the same direction for similar reasons, notably Asa Briggs, Alan Macfarlane, Raphael Samuel and Keith Thomas. I should also like to thank John Barnes, Tom Bottomore, Stefan Collini and Keith Hopkins for their comments on the draft. The book is dedicated to the sociologist from whom I have gained most.

1

Sociologists and Historians

A DIALOGUE OF THE DEAF

Sociologists and historians are not always the best of neighbours. Intellectual neighbours they certainly are, in the sense that both disciplines, together with social anthropology, are concerned with whole societies and with the full range of human behaviour. Sociology may be defined as the study of human society, with the emphasis on generalising about its structure. History may be defined as the study of human societies, with the emphasis on the differences between them and on the changes which have taken place in each one over time. The two approaches are obviously complementary. Change is structured, and structures change. It is only by comparing it with others that we can discover in what respects a given society is unique.

Each discipline can help to free the other from a kind of parochialism. Historians run the risk of parochialism in the more literal sense. Specialising as they do in a particular region and period, they may come to regard their 'parish' as unique territory, rather than as a unique combination of elements each of which has parallels elsewhere. Sociologists suffer from parochialism in a more metaphorical sense, a parochialism of time rather than place, whenever they generalise about 'society' on the basis of contemporary experience alone, or discuss social change over thirty years or so without looking at long-term processes as well.

Sociologists and historians each see the mote in their neighbour's eye. Unfortunately, each group tends to perceive the other in terms of a rather crude stereotype. In Britain at least, many historians still regard sociologists as people who state the obvious in a barbarous and abstract jargon, lack any sense of place or time, squeeze individuals into rigid categories and, to cap it all, believe that these activities are 'scientific'. Sociologists, for their part, see historians as amateurish myopic fact-collectors without a method, the vagueness of their data matched only by their incapacity to analyse them. In short, despite the existence of a few bilinguals whose work will often be mentioned in the pages which follow, sociologists and historians still do not speak the same language. Their dialogue, as the French historian Fernand Braudel has put it, is usually a 'dialogue of the deaf'.

It may be helpful to look at historians and sociologists from a sociological point of view, to see them not only as different professions but also as distinct subcultures, with their own languages, values and styles of thought, reinforced by their respective processes of training or 'socialisation'. Sociologists learn to turn to tables of figures, while many historians skip them and look for conclusions in words. Sociologists learn to notice rules and often screen out the exceptions, while historians are trained to attend to detail and often fail to see general patterns. A similar contrast has been drawn between the tribe of historians and the tribe of anthropologists (Cohn, 1962; Erikson, 1970; Dening, 1971 – 3).

From a historical point of view, it is clear that both parties are guilty of anachronism. Sociologists seem to think of history as if it were still in the Ranke phase of narrative without analysis; historians seem to think of sociology as if it were still in the Comte phase of grand generalisations without empirical research. Both subjects have changed a great deal since the middle of the nineteenth century. How and why did the two subcultures develop? The question is a historical one and in the next section I shall try to give it a historical answer. It will be a provisional answer, since a truly historical history of sociology has not yet been written (for the British part of the story, see Burrow, 1966; Collini, 1978).

THE DIFFERENTIATION OF HISTORY AND SOCIOLOGY

In the eighteenth century there were no disputes between sociologists and historians for a simple and obvious reason: sociology did not exist as a separate discipline. Montesquieu, Adam Ferguson and John Millar have since been claimed by sociologists; indeed, they are sometimes described as 'founding fathers' of sociology. This label is misleading (as it is when applied to Marx, Durkheim or Weber) because it gives the impression that these men set out to found a new subject. They never expressed any such intention.

It might be less misleading to describe Montesquieu, Ferguson and Millar as social theorists, because *The Spirit of the Laws* (1748), the *Essay on the History of Civil Society* (1767) and the *Observations on the Distinction of Ranks* (1771) are all comparative, analytical, and concerned not so much with political as with social theory, 'the philosophy of society' as Millar called it. However, one might equally well consider the trio to be analytical or, to use the eighteenth-century term, 'philosophical' historians. They all drew heavily on history for their illustrations, and all three wrote historical monographs: Montesquieu on the greatness and decline of Rome, Ferguson on the 'progress and termination of the Roman Republic' and Millar on the relation between government and society from the time of the Anglo-Saxons to the reign of Elizabeth I. In their generation, a number of writers were turning their backs on politics and war, the traditional subject-matter of history, to concern themselves with laws and customs ('manners' as they called them), commerce and the arts. For example, Voltaire's *Essay on Manners* (1756) dealt with social life in Europe from the time of Charlemagne. Voltaire's essay was not based directly on the sources, but it was a bold and original synthesis. By contrast, Justus Möser's *History of Osnabrück* (1768) was nothing if not scholarly, a local history written from the original documents. However, Möser had also read his Montesquieu and was encouraged

to relate the institutions of Westphalia to their environment
in an early example of the contribution of social theory to
historical research. Gibbon's *Decline and Fall* (1776 on)
was a social as well as a political history of the Roman
Empire which owes something to Adam Ferguson as well as
to Adam Smith.

A hundred years later, social theorists still remained
close to history. Marx discusses historical examples frequently and at length in *Capital* and elsewhere, while
Engels wrote a monograph on the German Peasants' War
of 1525. His monograph was not based on original
research, but the same criticism cannot be levelled at
Tocqueville's *The Old Regime and the French Revolution*,
which is a path-breaking history based on archives as well
as an important contribution to social theory.

Although Auguste Comte was much less interested in the
study of concrete historical situations than either
Tocqueville, Marx or Engels were, his life work might be
described as philosophy of history in the sense that it
attempted to identify the main trends in the past, which he
divided into three ages, the age of religion, the age of
metaphysics and the age of science. Comte believed that
social history, or, as he put it, 'history without the names
of individuals or even the names of peoples', was indispensable to the study of what he was the first to call
'sociology'. Herbert Spencer illustrated the process of
social evolution from the history of ancient Egypt, ancient
Greece, Russia under Peter the Great, and so on. The
'comparative method' practised by Marx, Comte, Spencer
and a number of their contemporaries was a historical
method in the sense that it involved placing every society,
and indeed every custom and artefact, in a time series
leading from 'savagery' to 'civilisation' (Nisbet, 1969,
ch. 6).

Historians, on the other hand, took social history rather
less seriously in 1850 than they had done in 1750. The most
revered historian of the period was Leopold von Ranke.
Ranke was not hostile to social history, but the books he
wrote, which were many, were focused on the state and had

little place for society. In his time and under his influence political history returned to its old position of dominance.

There were various reasons for this retreat from the social. The historical revolution associated with Ranke was a revolution in method which involved the attempt to write a more objective or 'scientific' history on the basis of official documents. Historians elaborated a set of sophisticated techniques for assessing the reliability of these documents. They knew how to organise their material when they had found it. There was a place for every fact and every fact was in its place – in a chronological sequence.

In contrast, the work of social historians looked unprofessional. 'Social history' is really too precise a term for what was in practice a residual category which G. M. Trevelyan would one day define quite explicitly as 'history with the politics left out'. The famous third chapter on society in the late seventeenth century in Macaulay's *History of England* (1848) was described by a contemporary reviewer, cruelly but not altogether unjustly, as an 'old curiosity shop', because the different topics – roads, marriage, newspapers, and so on – followed one another in no apparent order. Burckhardt's *Civilisation of the Renaissance in Italy* (1860), later recognised as a classic, was not a success at the time of publication, probably because it was an impressionistic essay based on literary sources and making little use of official documents. When J. R. Green published his *Short History of the English People* (1874), which concentrated on daily life at the expense of battles and treaties, his former tutor E. A. Freeman is said to have remarked that if Green had left out all that 'social stuff' he might have written a good history of England. The French historian Fustel de Coulanges, whose book *The Ancient City* (1860) was largely concerned with the history of the family in Greece and Rome, was relatively exceptional in being taken seriously by his professional colleagues while believing that history was the science of social facts, the true sociology.

In short, Ranke's historical revolution had one unintended but important consequence. Since the 'documents' approach worked best for traditional political history, its adoption made nineteenth-century historians narrower and even in a sense more old-fashioned in their choice of subject than their eighteenth-century predecessors. They rejected social history because it was not 'scientific' enough.

On the other hand, many historians rejected sociology because it was too scientific, in the sense that it was abstract and reductionist, that it did not allow for the uniqueness of individuals and events. This rejection was made articulate in the work of some late nineteenth-century German philosophers, such as Dilthey and Windelband. Dilthey, who was a practising cultural historian as well as a philosopher, considered the sociology of Comte and Spencer to be pseudo-scientific and drew the famous distinction between the sciences, which seek to explain from outside (*erklären*), and the humanities, including history, whose aim is to understand from within (*verstehen*) (Dilthey, 1883). Windelband drew the equally famous distinction between 'idiographic' history, concerned with the unique, and 'nomothetic' natural science, concerned with the establishing of general laws (Windelband, 1894). The leading English spokesman for this point of view, the philosopher-historian R. G. Collingwood, formulated the distinction between the historian and the scientist as follows (1935):

> When a scientist asks, 'Why did that piece of litmus paper turn pink?', he means 'On what kinds of occasions do pieces of litmus paper turn pink?'. When an historian asks, 'Why did Brutus stab Caesar?', he means, 'What did Brutus think, which made him stab Caesar?'.

On this view sociology is necessarily a pseudo-science, studying man by methods appropriate only to the study of nature, and there is no place for social history on the map of learning.

However, the hostile reaction to social history cannot be explained in intellectual terms alone. The dominance of political history in the nineteenth century (more precisely, its return to dominance) cries out for analysis in sociological terms. There are two obvious points to make here. Although 'historian' is a social role with a long history, stretching back to Herodotus if not further, the discipline was professionalised only in the nineteenth century, when the first research institutes, specialist journals and university departments were founded. It was then that the historians' guild rejected social history (as the sociologists' guild was to reject it a generation later) as incompatible with the new professional standards. The second point is that governments saw history as a means of promoting national unity, as education for citizenship, or, as a less sympathetic observer might have put it, as propaganda. At a time when the new states of Germany and Italy (and even older states like France and Spain) were divided by local traditions, the teaching of national history in schools and universities fulfilled the function of social integration. The kind of history for which governments were prepared to pay was, naturally enough, the history of the state. The links between history and the government were particularly strong in Germany (Gilbert, 1965; Moses, 1975).

Social theorists, for their part, continued to study history, but they had little time for historians. Comte, for example, referred with contempt to the 'insignificant details so childishly collected by the irrational curiosity of the blind compilers of sterile anecdotes' (Comte, 1864, lecture 52). Herbert Spencer declared that sociology stood to history 'much as a vast building stands related to the heaps of stones and bricks around it'. Again: 'The highest office which the historian can discharge is that of so narrating the lives of nations, as to furnish materials for a Comparative Sociology.' We have moved a long way from the eighteenth-century co-operation between philosophical historians and philosophers of society. At best the historians were seen as collectors of raw material for sociologists. At worst they were totally irrelevant because they did not even heap up the right kind of brick. To quote Spencer once more: 'The biographies of monarchs (and our children learn little else) throw scarcely any light upon the science of society' (Spencer, 1911, pp. 26 – 9).

In the early twentieth century the major social theorists still took history seriously, whatever they thought of historians. Like Comte and Spencer before him, Emile Durkheim seems to have thought that much historical work was really 'vain erudition'. However, he also believed that the past could be of use to sociology, and he drew on the work of Fustel de Coulanges, under whom he had studied at the Ecole Normale, in his books *The Division of Labour* (1893) and *The Elementary Forms of the Religious Life* (1912). Durkheim himself wrote a history of education in France. He made it the policy of his journal, the *Année sociologique*, to review books on history, provided they were not concerned with what he called the 'superficial' history of events. It is likely that he would have approved of the French historians such as Lucien Febvre and Marc Bloch who themselves rejected the history of events a generation later (Bellah, 1959; Momigliano, 1970; Lukes, 1973, ch. 2).

As for Max Weber, the breadth and depth of his historical knowledge were truly phenomenal. He wrote books on the trading companies of the Middle Ages and the agrarian history of Rome before making his famous study of the Protestant ethic and the spirit of capitalism. The great classical scholar Theodor Mommsen considered Weber a worthy successor. When he turned to the theory of economic and social organisation, Weber did not give up the study of the past. He drew on history for material and on historians for concepts, like 'patrimonial state' or 'charisma', a term which he took from a discussion of the early church by the ecclesiastical historian Rudolph Sohm and gave a more general application. It was appropriate that the most historically minded of the great sociologists should have come from the most historically minded nation in Europe. In fact, Weber scarcely thought of himself as a sociologist at all. At the end of his life, when he had accepted a chair in the subject at Munich, he made the dry comment, 'I now happen to be a sociologist according to my appointment papers' (Bendix, 1960; Mommsen, 1974; Roth, 1976).

Durkheim and Weber did not stand alone among the sociologists of their day in their interest in history. Tönnies, for example, was trained as a classicist and retained his interest in the past. Pareto's treatise on sociology discussed classical Athens, Rome and Sparta at considerable length and also took examples from the history of Italy in the Middle Ages. Albion Small, who became chairman of the first sociology department in the United States (at Chicago, in 1892), had previously been a professor of history. Like Durkheim and Spencer, Small was critical of the historical profession but continued to study the past. The new discipline of anthropology was also close to history at this time. Sir James Frazer, who held the first chair in social anthropology in Britain (as visiting professor at Liverpool in 1907 – 8), was an ex-classicist turned comparative historian of primitive thought. In the United States, Franz Boas, who founded the first university departments of anthropology (at Clark in 1888 and at Columbia in 1899), thought of his subject as concerned with the 'culture histories' of different tribes as a basis for generalisations about the evolution of mankind.

Then, quite suddenly, about the year 1920, anthropologists and sociologists broke with the past. The British-trained anthropologist Bronislaw Malinowski discovered and proclaimed the importance of 'field work' as he called it; in other words, participant observation. Such participant observation was not completely new; Boas had been making long visits to the Kwakiutl since 1886, and Radcliffe-Brown spent the years 1906 – 8 in the Andaman Islands. What was new was Malinowski's insistence on fieldwork as the anthropological method *par excellence*. 'The anthropologist', he declared, 'must relinquish his comfortable position in the long chair on the veranda.' Fieldwork became a necessary stage in the training of every anthropologist. The new method, like Ranke's history, was more scientific; a more reliable way of studying contemporary tribal societies than the largely conjectural evolutionary history which had preceded it. However, it could not be applied to the past.

Sociologists too began to take more and more of their data from contemporary society, whether they used official statistics or carried out their own surveys. Durkheim's *Suicide* (1897) is an example of the first of these approaches; the work of the Chicago school in the 1920s illustrates the second. Members of the sociology department of the University of Chicago studied the city, especially its slums, in the 'field' as if they were social anthropologists. The leaders of this project, Robert Park and Ernest Burgess, were consciously emulating Franz Boas. Their method was soon imitated by sociologists elsewhere.

There were several reasons for this fundamental shift to the cultivation of the present at the expense of the past. One reason was practical. Since historians had not furnished sociologists with the raw material they needed, sociologists were obliged to make their bricks themselves. The more material they collected and the more monographs they published, the easier it was to theorise on the basis of their own studies, and the harder it was to find time to read outside 'their' area. The discipline was becoming institutionalised, professionalised. The greater the professional self-consciousness of sociologists, the less they wanted to depend on 'alien' material, whether ethnographical or historical.

These changes within the discipline coincided with some more general intellectual developments. Explanations of customs or social institutions by the past, in terms of social evolution and social diffusion, were replaced by explanations of the social functions of these customs and institutions in the present. Historical explanations were first criticised as speculative and then dismissed as irrelevant. Durkheim had combined a functionalist approach with an interest in history, but later functionalists, like Malinowski, dropped history altogether. According to him, the past was 'dead and buried', and only the image of the past mattered, because this image was part of 'the psychological reality of today' (Malinowski, 1946, ch. 3). To slip for a moment into functionalist language, one might say that functionalism 'fitted in well' with the new methods of fieldwork. The new approach spread from anthropology to sociology and came to dominate it, in the United States in particular. The attempt to make sociology a 'behavioral science', to use a fashionable American term of the 1950s, a discipline which counted and measured wherever it was possible (and sometimes, one is tempted to add, when it was not), only increased the distance between sociologists and historians.

There was no point at which sociologists gave up studying history altogether. In the 1920s, for example, Karl Mannheim's sociology of knowledge was historical in method. In the 1930s, Robert Merton was investigating the links between puritanism and science in seventeenth-century England, a case study in the tradition of Max Weber, while Norbert Elias, a follower of Mannheim, was writing his great study *The Civilising Process*, a book which may perhaps best be described as a sociological interpretation of European history from the Middle Ages onwards. In 1941, George Homans published a book entitled *English Villagers of the Thirteenth Century*. All these studies were important, but their authors were swimming against the stream.

Ironically enough, the sociologists lost interest in the past at just the time that historians were beginning to produce something like the 'natural history of society' which Spencer had called for.

THE RISE OF SOCIAL HISTORY

At the end of the nineteenth century some professional historians were unhappy with the dominance of the political. One of the most vocal was Karl Lamprecht, who criticised the German historical establishment for its emphasis on political history and on the history of great men, and called for a 'collective history' which would draw on other disciplines for its concepts. The other disciplines included the social psychology of Wundt (under whom both Durkheim and Malinowski studied), and the 'human geography' of Ratzel, both colleagues of Lamprecht's at the University of Leipzig. 'History', declared Lamprecht, with characteristic boldness, 'is primarily a socio-psychological science.' He put this socio-psychological approach into practice in his multi-volume *History of Germany* (1891 – 1909), which was favourably reviewed in Durkheim's *Année sociologique* but was not so much criticised as mocked by orthodox German historians, for its inaccuracies (which were in fact numerous), and for its so-called 'materialism' and 'reductionism'. Lamprecht's sometimes crude formulations were indeed open to criticism. However, the violence of the 'Lamprecht controversy', as it came to be called, suggests that his real sin was to have called Rankean history into question. The administrative historian Otto Hintze was unusual in making specific criticisms of Lamprecht but accepting the kind of history he advocated as 'progress beyond Ranke', on the grounds that 'we want to know not only the ranges and summits but also the base of the mountains, not merely the heights and depths of the surface but the entire continental mass' (Hintze, 1897).

Around 1900, most German historians did not think in terms of going beyond Ranke. When Max Weber was making his study of Protestantism and capitalism, he was able to draw on the work of some German colleagues who were interested in similar problems, but it may be significant that the most important of them, Werner Sombart and Ernst Troeltsch, occupied chairs, not in history, but in economics and theology.

Lamprecht failed in Germany, but in the United States and in France the campaign for social history met with greater success. The American historian Frederick Jackson Turner launched an attack on the dominance of political history in the 1890s. 'All the spheres of man's activity must be considered', he wrote 'No one department of social life can be understood in isolation from the others.' Like Lamprecht, Turner had been impressed by Ratzel's human geography. His essay 'The significance of the frontier in American history' was a controversial but epoch-making interpretation of American institutions as a response to a particular geographical and social environment. Elsewhere he discussed the importance in American history of what he called 'sections', in other words regions, like New England or the Middle West, with their own economic interests and their own resources (Turner, 1891, 1893, 1904).

Turner's contemporary, James Harvey Robinson, was another eloquent preacher of what he called 'the new history', a history concerned with social trends and open to the social sciences. Robinson's friend Charles Beard was inspired by Turner – and by Marx – to write his famous, and once again controversial, *Economic Interpretation of the Constitution of the United States* (1913), in which he argued that 'the line of cleavage for and against the constitution was between substantial personality interests on the one hand and the small farming and debtor interests on the other'. That social history has had an established place in the United States since the 1920s is suggested by the multi-volume *History of American Life*, edited by Arthur Schlesinger, Snr, which began publication in 1927.

In France, too, there was a confrontation between historians and social scientists at the beginning of the century, when an economist, François Simiand, launched an attack on what he called the three 'idols of the tribe' of historians, the idol of politics, the idol of the individual and the idol of chronology, and denounced in particular the traditional emphasis on the history of events (*histoire événementielle*, as he called it, with some contempt; Simiand, 1903). He was answered by Charles Seignobos, who declared that 'history is the science of the unique' (*l'histoire est la science de ce qui n'arrive qu'une fois*); the coupling of the emphasis on science and the rejection of generalisation is characteristic of historians of this period. However, Simiand's ideas were taken seriously by some leading members of the next generation of French historians.

In the 1920s, a movement for a 'new kind of history' got under way, led by two professors at the University of Strasbourg, Lucien Febvre and Marc Bloch, who founded a journal to encourage their kind of history and called it *Annales d'histoire economique et sociale*. Like Lamprecht

and Turner, Febvre and Bloch disliked the dominance of
political history. They wanted to replace it with a 'wider
and more human history', a history which would include all
human activities and which would be less concerned with
the narrative of events than with the analysis of
'structures', a term which has since become a favourite
with French historians. Febvre and Bloch both wanted
historians to learn from neighbouring disciplines. Febvre,
like Lamprecht, was particularly interested in social
psychology and human geography, though he was much
less of a determinist. He read Ratzel, but rejected him for
the more voluntarist approach of the great French geo-
grapher Vidal de la Blache. Bloch was more interested in
the sociology of Durkheim, and shared his interests in
social solidarity and 'collective representations' (see below,
p.75), and his commitment to a comparative method.
Bloch was shot by the Germans in 1944, but Febvre survived the Second World War to take over the French
historical establishment and indeed the social science
establishment as well, as president of the newly formed
Ecole des Hautes Etudes en Sciences Sociales (on the
'Annales School', Hughes, 1969, pt 1; Iggers, 1975, ch. 1).

Febvre handed over to Fernand Braudel, a historian who
believes that history and sociology should be specially close
because the practitioners of both disciplines try, or ought
to try, to see human experience as a whole (Braudel, 1955).
Braudel's *Mediterranean World in the Age of Philip II*
(1949), a 'total history' (*histoire globale*) dealing with geography, society and politics, with structures and events, has
a good claim to be regarded as the most important work of
history of the century (see below, p.94). Their association
in the Ecole des Hautes Etudes, founded in 1948, allowed a
dialogue between French sociologists, anthropologists and
historians at a time when this was difficult elsewhere. All
the same, French historians, unlike their American colleagues, seem to have learned much more from geographers
than they have from sociologists (Planhol, 1972).

France and the United States are two countries where
social history has been taken seriously for a relatively long

time and where relations between sociology and history have been particularly close. This is not to say that nothing of this kind was going on elsewhere. The Japanese, for example, have an important tradition of social history. Eijirō Honjō, to choose a historian who published in English, was at work in the 1930s on the social history of Tokugawa Japan. In Brazil there was Gilberto Freyre, an amphibian who can equally well be described as a sociologist or a historian. Freyre's study *The Masters and the Slaves* (1933), concerned with the plantation society of his native north-east, has become a classic. In Britain social history came into the universities attached to the coat tails of economic history, and it is not completely accepted even yet, but J. L. and Barbara Hammond's important study *The Village Labourer*, to take just one example, goes back to 1911. In their separate departments, a few classicists (notably Jane Harrison) drew on the ideas of sociologists and anthropologists such as Durkheim and Frazer to reinterpret the history of Greek culture.

In this brief account of the rise of social history, one obvious name has been deliberately omitted: that of Marx. Despite Marx's own interest in history, already discussed, Marxism does not seem to have made a serious impact on the writing of history in the West until the 1950s (I am excluding developments in the USSR). Despite obvious similarities between his historical interests and theirs, in total history and in the relations between structures and events, Marx does not appear to have been taken seriously by Febvre, Bloch, or even by Braudel when he was writing his *Mediterranean*. In the first half of the twentieth century, only a few leading historians were Marxists, among them Halvdan Koht, whose book on peasant risings in Norway was published in 1926, and Jan Romein, whose social history of the Netherlands came out in 1934.

THE CONVERGENCE OF SOCIOLOGY AND HISTORY

It is clear that by the middle of the twentieth century a sizeable corpus of social history had accumulated, which sociologists could have used had they wanted. However, it was only in the 1950s, and more obviously in the 1960s, that sociology and history began to converge. In 1954, two American sociologists founded a committee for 'the socio-logical study of historical documents'. They did this because their interest in history made them, so they put it, 'lonely and isolated' among their professional colleagues (Cahnman and Boskoff, 1964, introduction). They did not remain isolated for long. Talcott Parsons, who had once asked 'Who reads Spencer now?', became interested in an evolutionary model of social change. Two of the best-known monographs on history written by American socio-logists originated as theses under his supervision: Robert Bellah's *Tokugawa Religion* (1957), a search for the Japanese equivalent of the protestant ethic, and Neil Smelser's *Social Change in the Industrial Revolution* (1959), which deals with the family structure and working conditions of Lancashire weavers in the early nineteenth century.

A trickle in the 1950s, historical sociology is now a stream. S. M. Lipset's *The First New Nation* (1963), Charles Tilly's *The Vendée* (1964), Barrington Moore's *Social Origins of Dictatorship and Democracy* (1966) and Immanuel Wallerstein's *The Modern World System* (1974) are among the more celebrated American contributions. Some social anthropologists have moved in the same direc-tion. Eric Wolf's *Peasant Wars* (1969) and Anton Blok's *The Mafia of a Sicilian Village* (1974) are examples.

There are obvious reasons for this return to history. Accelerating social change virtually forced itself on the attention of sociologists. There has also been time, since its adoption in the 1920s, to work through the functionalist approach and discover its deficiencies, such as the danger of studying social life from outside without taking into account the intentions of the 'actors' or their definitions of the situation. Sociologists who concern themselves with the actor's point of view, whether they call themselves 'phenomenologists', 'symbolic interactionists', or what-ever, are much closer than the functionalists to historians who have never ceased trying to look at the past through the eyes of contemporaries. A historian is tempted to comment that sociologists have just discovered for themselves what historians were doing all the time, but has also to admit that with characteristic thoroughness, the sociologists are now taking the approach further.

Social anthropologists, for their part, have always been interested in the concepts of the peoples they study, but the rapid social changes of the last generation have made them, like sociologists, more concerned with processes of change over time.

Meanwhile historians have been turning to social history and taking an interest in sociology. Despite the efforts of some members of the guild, the rising tide of social history could not be kept back, and here too a sociological explanation may be in order. In order to orient themselves in a period of rapid social change, some people have found it useful to take a closer look at the past – the social past.

The rise of social history has made the question 'what is social history?' an increasingly urgent one. When political history was dominant, it was perhaps sufficient to define social history as history with the politics left out. Such a residual definition is no longer useful. This residual social history has often been criticised as an 'invertebrate' subject, lacking a framework or structure, in other words without a means of linking different pieces of information about social life in the past into a coherent description, narrative or analysis. This was the point of the contemporary criticism of Macaulay's social history as an 'old curiosity shop', and also of the milder but no less cogent criticisms of the *History of American Life* series (Perkin, 1953; Hofstadter, 1968). Hence recent calls for a more rigorous social history defined in more positive terms, whether it is called 'social structural history' or 'the history of society' or whatever (Laslett, 1968; Hobsbawm, 1971b).

Historians who are interested in this more rigorous social history have been borrowing concepts and methods from sociology and from social anthropology. A few of them have taken up the concept of 'function', ironically enough, as so often happens in interdisciplinary relations, at the very time when sociologists and anthropologists are considering abandoning it. Many historians are now interested in quantitative methods, which have spread outwards from economic history (the 'new economic history' or 'cliometrics'), again at a time when the virtues of counting have ceased to be taken for granted by social scientists and have become the subject of debate.

What is to be done? At this point it is time for me to reveal my own values, my own bias. I believe that social history is a valuable as well as a fascinating enterprise, as worthy of serious study as its older sisters political and economic history, as necessary to understanding the present as its cousins sociology and social anthropology. The story I have tried to tell of the split between history and sociology is a 'what went wrong?' story. To say this is not to dismiss the very great achievements of the Ranke school of political historians and the Malinowski school of functionalist anthropologists and sociologists. It is simply to draw attention to the fact that there was a price to pay for these achievements, a price which there is no need to go on paying. What some of us would like to see, what we are beginning to see, is a social history, or historical sociology – the distinction should become irrelevant – which would be concerned both with understanding from within and explaining from without; with the general and with the particular; and which would combine the sociologist's acute sense of structure with the historian's equally sharp sense of change. It is to encourage this synthesis of what have too often been separate and even conflicting approaches that I have written this essay. The following chapters will attempt to specify, as concretely and as precisely as possible, what historians and sociologists can learn from one another.

2

Social Structures

There are a number of definitions of social history which are more positive than 'history with the politics left out'. It might be defined as the history of social relationships; the history of the social structure; the history of everyday life; the history of private life; the history of social solidarities and social conflicts; the history of social classes; the history of social groups 'seen both as separate and as mutually dependent units' (on the last definition, see Rüter, 1956). These definitions are very far from being synonymous; each corresponds to a different approach, with its advantages and disadvantages. But it is difficult to take any of these approaches very far without some acquaintance with the concepts of sociology, with its language.

We have returned to the problem of the 'jargon' which historians often accuse sociologists of writing and even speaking. British intellectuals are perhaps more prone than most, thanks to the survival of the tradition of the gentlemanly amateur, to accuse one another of this sin. 'Jargon' here means little more than the other man's concepts. Assuming that every divergence from ordinary language has its price, because it makes communication with the general reader more difficult; assuming that every divergence from ordinary language is in need of justification, there remains a minimum of technical terms from sociology which historians, especially social historians, would be well advised to admit into their vocabulary. Some of these terms have no equivalent in ordinary language – and if we have no word for something, it is all too easy not to notice it at all. Others are defined more precisely than their equivalents in ordinary language and so enable one to make finer distinctions and so a more rigorous analysis than ordinary language allows.

The primary aim of this chapter is therefore to offer historians who think they need it an elementary phrasebook of the language of sociology, or, to vary the metaphor, a basic conceptual tool kit suitable for some of the more common breakdowns in historical analysis. Since the proof of a concept's value lies in its application, each term will be discussed as it has been used or might be used to study concrete historical problems. Examples will usually be taken from the history of Europe in the sixteenth and seventeenth centuries. There are several reasons for this choice. It is the period with which I am most familiar; it is the period on which the French historians associated with *Annales* have most often written (see above, p.25); and it is a relatively well-documented group of pre-industrial societies. Since the concepts of sociology were created for the most part after the industrial revolution, to examine them in a pre-industrial context should test the limits of their applicability and even possibly reveal the cracks in the theoretical structure. In other words, this chapter is intended for sociologists as well as for historians, on the assumption that it takes a foreigner to notice the limitations of a language.

Of course the linguistic metaphor must not be pushed too far. Sociology is not just a vocabulary, a storehouse of useful, neutral conceptual tools. It is a discipline whose practitioners disagree strongly about what to do and how to do it. Indeed, it is difficult to think of an objection to any approach in sociology which a sociologist has not already made. Any historian who thinks sociologists are all smugly uncritical speakers of unintelligible jargon should read C. Wright Mills's famous assault on the 'Grand Theory' and the 'Abstracted Empiricism' of some of his professional colleagues (Mills, 1959). Any historian who thinks that sociologists are all positivists in white coats treating their objects of study as things rather than as people with ideas and theories of their own should read some of the work of the 'interpretative' or 'phenomenological' sociologists or the 'ethnomethodologists' (Berger, 1963; Turner, 1974).

THE COMPARATIVE METHOD

Sociology can offer the historian not only concepts but methods: survey analysis, network analysis, content analysis, and so on. One of the most important of these methods is the comparative method.

Traditional historians have often objected to borrowing from sociology on the grounds that the two disciplines have opposite aims. Sociology is concerned with the establishment of general laws, while history is concerned with the particular, the unrepeatable, the unique (Collingwood, 1935; Elton, 1967, pp. 23f.; above, p.18). To this classic objection there is an equally classic answer, given by Max Weber in 1914 to the conservative German historian Georg von Below: 'We are absolutely in accord that history should establish what is specific, say, to the mediaeval city; but this is possible only if we first find what is missing in other cities (ancient, Chinese, Islamic)' (quoted in Roth, 1976, p. 307). In other words, the historical and the sociological approaches are both complementary and dependent on one another, and both necessarily involve the comparative method. One might say that comparisons are useful primarily because they enable us to see what is not there. Comparisons are also useful in the search for explanations. To see what varies with what makes it easier to understand the differences between one society and another. It was for this reason that Durkheim called the comparative method a kind of 'indirect experiment', without which it would be impossible to move from description to analysis. He distinguished two main kinds of comparison, between societies which were fundamentally the same in structure and between societies which were fundamentally different, but he considered both procedures to be of value (Durkheim, 1895, ch. 6). Weber too practised the comparative method as well as preaching it to Georg von Below. Indeed, he spent much of his working life in the attempt to define the distinctive characteristics of Western civilisation by means of systematic comparisons, notably comparisons between Europe and Asia. Unlike the comparisons of Comte, Marx and Spencer, Weber's approach did not presuppose any unilinear social 'evolution' (see pp82, 86 below).

A few leading historians of the early twentieth century learned the comparative method from the sociologists. The Prussian historian Otto Hintze, who made a number of comparative studies, including one of the *commissarius* (an official removable at the ruler's will) in different European states, was inspired by Weber, for whose work he had considerable admiration (Hintze, 1919). Marc Bloch learned the comparative method from Durkheim. He defined it in a similar way, distinguishing comparisons between neighbouring societies from comparisons between societies remote from one another in space and time. He advocated it on similar grounds, because it allowed the historian 'to take a real step forward in the exciting search for causes'. Among his best-known comparative studies are his investigation of touching for the 'king's evil' in France and England in the Middle Ages, and the section on Japan in his book on feudal society in Europe. Bloch argued that Japan, like Western Europe, passed through a feudal 'phase', though he was at pains to emphasise the difference between the bilateral obligations between lord and vassal in Europe and the unilateral obligations which bound the samurai to his master (Bloch, 1923, 1928, 1939 – 40, bk 3).

A more ambitious but much less successful comparative study is Arnold Toynbee's massive *Study of History* (1935 – 61). The tragedy of this heroic attempt at comparative history on the global scale is, to my mind at least, Toynbee's lack of an adequate conceptual apparatus. Terms like 'challenge and response', 'withdrawal and return', 'universal state' and 'external proletariat' have their uses, but proved to be insufficient tools for the job. If only Toynbee had read Max Weber ... but Weber does not seem to have had much impact on England in the 1920s and 1930s. Some historians, R. H. Tawney, for example, were aware of Weber as the author of a stimulating if rash essay on the Protestant ethic and the spirit of capitalism, but his major works do not seem to have been well known. R. G. Collingwood, like Toynbee, seems to have been unaware of Weber's work, despite its relevance to his own. Collingwood theorised about history as the study of the unique as if comparative history, social history and even the longer-established economic history did not exist in his day. After all, economic and social historians often generalise. Even when they are not comparing one society with another, they make general statements about particular places at particular times. They try to explain why prices rose in sixteenth-century Spain, why men went into Parliament in eighteenth-century England, and so on. Like sociologists, they make use of models and types.

HISTORY, MODELS AND TYPES

Let us define a 'model' in simple terms as an intellectual construct which simplifies reality in order to emphasise the recurrent, the constant and the typical, which it presents in the form of clusters of traits or attributes. In other words, 'models' and 'types' are treated as synonyms. Traditional historians often deny having anything to do with models, but in practice many of them use models as M. Jourdain used prose, without realising that they do so. Avoiding the word 'model', they nevertheless allow themselves to use general terms like 'feudalism' and 'capitalism', 'Renaissance' and 'Enlightenment', or to talk about the 'classical' or the 'textbook' form of a social phenomenon like the mediaeval manor. Using models in this way without being aware of their logical status has sometimes landed historians in needless difficulties. Some well-known debates within the profession have turned on one historian's misunderstanding of another historian's model.

One example of such a misunderstanding is the celebrated controversy between Sir Paul Vinogradoff and F. W. Maitland about the mediaeval English manor. Vinogradoff (1892, pp. 223 − 4) suggested that

The structure of the ordinary manor is always the same.

> Under the headship of the lord we find two layers of
> population – the villeins and the freeholders, and the
> territory occupied divides itself accordingly into demesne
> land and 'tributary land'... The entire population is
> grouped into a village community which centres round
> the manorial court or halimote, which is both council
> and tribunal. My investigation will necessarily conform
> to this typical arrangement.

This is the 'classic' mediaeval manor as it has been drawn
on innumerable blackboards. In an equally classic piece of
destructive analysis, Maitland argued that 'to describe a
typical *manerium* is an impossible feat' and showed that
each of the traits in the cluster identified by Vinogradoff
was lacking in some instances. Some manors had no
villeins, others no freeholders, others no demesne, others
no court (Maitland, 1897).

Vinogradoff appears to have been uncertain about the
logical status of his generalisations (note the shift from
'always' in the first sentence quoted to 'typical' in the last).
If he had been more aware that he was using a model, he
might have made more cautious claims and he would also
have been able to give a convincing reply to Maitland.

It is useful to distinguish two kinds of model according
to the criteria for membership in the group of entities, in
this case manors, to which the model applies. Jargon is
unavoidable here. We need to distinguish a 'monothetic'
group of entities from a 'polythetic' group. A monothetic
group is a group 'so defined that the possession of a unique
set of attributes is both sufficient and necessary for
membership'. A polythetic group, on the other hand, is a
group in which no single attribute is either necessary or
sufficient for group membership. The group is defined in
terms of a set of attributes such that each entity possesses
most of the attributes and each attribute is shared by most
of the entities (Clarke, 1968, p. 37). This second situation is
of course the one described by Wittgenstein in a famous
passage on 'family resemblances'. Mothers and sons,
brothers and sisters resemble one another, yet these

resemblances may not be reducible to any one essential feature.

Maitland's objections to Vinogradoff assumed that Vinogradoff was talking about all manors or defining the 'typical' manor with reference to a monothetic group. Vinogradoff could have replied, had the concept been available, by saying that his model was a polythetic one. The onus would then have been on him to show that each of the attributes in his cluster was shared by most manors. This cannot be done for the whole of England, but when a Russian historian studied manors in Cambridgeshire and neighbouring counties in the thirteenth century, he found that over 50 per cent of them were of what he called 'type A', with demesne, villein land and freeholdings – in other words, Vinogradoff's type (Kosminsky, 1935).

Like sociologists, social historians cannot do without the concept of the 'typical'. When they make their typologies, both groups are of course following the example of natural scientists. They are doing 'taxonomy' and distinguishing 'species', just as Linnaeus did with his plants. However, the different species of mediaeval manor are less visible than (say) the different species of eucalyptus. To discover whether or not a given case is 'representative', and if so, of what group it is typical, the social historian needs to practise what the sociologists call 'survey analysis'.

SURVEY ANALYSIS

Survey analysis both is and is not what social historians do all the time without necessarily knowing it. The English House of Commons and the Roman Senate have been studied through the biographies of their members, 'collective biography' or 'prosopography', as this method is sometimes called. In these cases, the whole group, or as sociologists would say, the 'total population', has been studied as far as the surviving records would permit. In such cases, acquaintance with the methods of survey analysis practised in neighbouring disciplines may not be necessary. Historians of elites and historians of pre-industrial societies in which statistics are neither plentiful nor reliable are well advised to proceed by collecting all the data they can find.

However, contemporary historians, and historians concerned with large groups, like the British working class, or with whole societies, tend to have access to more information than they can handle, and for them survey analysis and sampling methods may have some use. Gilberto Freyre, for example, writing the history of Brazil in the late nineteenth and early twentieth centuries, has tried to find a thousand Brazilians born between 1850 and 1900 who would represent the main social groups within the nation, though he does not explain by what method this sample was selected (Freyre, 1959; cf. Skidmore, 1964). Paul Thompson, whose social history of Edwardian England is largely based on interviews with 500 surviving Edwardians, picked people for interview on the basis of a 'quota sample', which provided a balance between men and women, town and country, north and south, and so on, similar to the balance prevailing in the whole country at the time (Thompson, 1975, pp. 5 – 8).

Freyre and Thompson are as much sociologists as historians and they have made their surveys of the living, but the problem of sampling recurs in historical surveys of the dead. Gerald Aylmer's study of Charles I's civil service is concerned with about 900 men studied through a sample of 194. His study of the civil servants of the English Republic deals with about 1,180 officials via a random sample of 284 of them. In this case the numbers involved made a total prosopography unsuitable for a one-man study. Lawrence Stone was able to study all the English peers between 1558 and 1641 because there were only 382 of them; Gerald Aylmer, who had over 2,000 officials to deal with, was forced to sample (Aylmer, 1961, 1973; Stone, 1965).

A social survey of the past, like a social survey of the present, raises two awkward problems. There is the problem of the reliability of the evidence, or 'data', and there is the problem of categorising it or them.

The essential reliability problem for anyone using

quantitative methods is the well known one of the difference between 'hard' (precise, measurable) data and 'soft' data which are the reverse. 'All too often it is the soft data which are valuable, and the hard which are relatively easy to get.' Like sociologists, historians need to find 'hard facts which can be relied upon to serve as good indices of soft ones' (Wootton, 1959, p. 311). An 'index' may be defined as something measurable which varies ('co-varies') with something which is not.

In the 1930s, for example, American sociologists discovered that the type of house a given family lived in, and even the furnishings of their living room, correlated well with income and occupation and could therefore be taken as an index of that family's social status. On the 'living room scale', a telephone or a radio, for example, scored high ($+8$), while an alarm clock scored very low (-2). Given the number of inventories which survive from early modern Europe, Chapin's living room scale opens up vistas for social historians (Chapin, 1935, ch. 19). Or would such an index be reliable only for the USA in the 1930s? Presumably the accuracy of a scale like this depends on the preoccupation with status and its symbols in a given culture. On these grounds, one might have expected the scale to apply even better to Europe in the seventeenth century than to the United States in the twentieth, making due allowance for changes in house furnishings. However, we learn from the literature of the period that the status symbols of the seventeenth century were somewhat different. In Furetière's *Roman bourgeois*, for example, where the story revolves round some young lawyers who try to pass themselves off as nobles, there are occasional references to furnishings (suggesting that in those days antique furniture was an indicator of poverty, meanness or old-fashioned attitudes rather than high status or good taste). However, the true indices of status, according to the literature, were clothes. It is by ribbons and lace that Furetière's bourgeois heroes pass for courtiers. The literature of the picaresque in seventeenth-century Spain confirms the importance of clothes as the central status symbol

(Furetière, 1666). There is a moral for historians here. It is the concept of an index which they may usefully borrow from sociologists, but not any specific index.

Sociologists of religion have had to deal with an even more acute problem, that of finding an index to measure the intensity or the orthodoxy of religious belief. They have tended to fasten on the proportion of clergy in a given population, church or chapel attendance figures, or, in Catholic countries like France and Italy, the numbers of Easter communicants (Le Bras, 1955; Wilson, 1966). One ingenious French historian has even tried to calculate the decline of devotion in eighteenth-century Provence from the falling weight of candles burned before the images of the saints (Vovelle, 1973). There is little doubt that statistics of this kind, which vary greatly between one region and another and change a good deal, sometimes quite sharply, over time, have a story to tell. Whether we can read that story is another matter. To read the figures correctly would involve knowing exactly what Easter communion meant to the people involved; it is difficult to be sure whether or not the peasants of the Orléans region in the nineteenth century (say) held the orthodox clerical view of communion or not. To take the religious temperature of a community, whether it is cold or hot or lukewarm, is more difficult than it may look. The problems of inferring political attitudes from voting figures are of the same order.

Hard or soft, the data will not furnish answers to our questions unless they are 'fitted', with a greater or less degree of squeezing, into categories. Historians cannot afford to feel superior to sociologists in this respect. We all use categories, and we would not be able to reach any conclusions at all without them. We all have to squeeze on occasion, however much we try to construct categories which will do the least violence to the data while enabling conclusions to be reached. To use the quantitative methods involved in survey analysis does not introduce categories for the first time; it simply makes the business of classification more self-conscious than usual. The computer will only take a straight 'yes' or 'no' for an answer. If a historian wants to make use of a computer or card-sorter, he has to code his data in such a way that they can be punched on to IBM cards or on to tape. (Although technological changes are putting it out of date, the best introduction to this subject remains Shorter, 1971, ch. 2.)

For an example of the kinds of problem involved in coding historical evidence, it is convenient to draw on my own work on the collective biography of 600 artists and writers who were active in Renaissance Italy. Neither the total creative population (which would be impossible to define), nor a random sample, the 600 were chosen as the best-known workers in their respective fields, their names being taken from standard modern works of reference. It might be argued that it would have been better to pick the 600 people most famous at the time, rather than the 600 people of the time most famous now; in other words, more canon lawyers and theologians and fewer painters. However, this choice would have been inappropriate given the original problem, which was to explain the extraordinary flourishing of talent in what we call the Italian Renaissance. The quantitative approach simply forced me to make explicit the implicit criteria of selection of other modern historians. After selecting the names, the next step was to collect information about each individual and to write it on record cards. The third step was to code the information; that is, to select the questions to be asked (ten questions in this case), and to categorise the possible answers in 'punchable' form. To the question 'Where was X born?', for example, there were nine possible answers, ranging from 'Tuscany' (punch a hole in the first position in the first column), to 'not known' (ninth position in the first column). To the question 'What was the occupation of X's father?' there were again nine answers, from 'nobleman' to 'not known', and so on. There were in all sixty-three possible answers to the ten questions, and the computer, fitted with a standard survey analysis programme, printed out the sixty-three categories horizontally and vertically, so that to find out how many Tuscans in the group were the sons of noblemen, one simply took a reading along the two axes.

A point deserving emphasis is the difficulty, in some cases, of deciding which category was the appropriate one to punch. Is Michelangelo's father (say) better described as 'noble' or as 'professional'? One has to choose. If in the case of a particular category the marginal cases pile up and the choices seem arbitrary, then it is better not to use that category at all. I had planned a question about the psychology of artists and writers, using sixteenth-century categories like 'melancholic', but abandoned it on just these grounds. 'Born in Tuscany' is a hard fact, susceptible to quantitative treatment without distortion; 'melancholic' is a soft one, dependent on the attitudes, values and prejudices of the source (Burke, 1972, ch. 3).

STRUCTURE AND FUNCTION

Two key words in the vocabulary of sociologists are 'structure' and 'function'. 'Structure' or 'system' (the terms will not be distinguished here) refers to an entity composed of mutually dependent parts. To speak of the 'social structure' of seventeenth-century England, say, is to suggest that the major institutions (king, church, Parliament, guilds, manors, and so on), and the major groups in society (peers, gentry, yeomen, craftsmen, and so on) depended on one another, in the sense that a change in one group or institution would be followed by changes in others. In a sense the historian ought not to find anything strange about this idea; historians, like sociologists, tend to expect everything in society to be somehow connected with everything else. However, they may well be a little suspicious of the concept 'structure' in its more precise sense, particularly when it is combined with 'function'. 'Function', too, is an apparently harmless concept which may suggest no more than that institutions have their uses; but defined more precisely, there is a cutting edge to it which makes the concept at once more interesting and more dangerous. The function of each part of society, so the definition goes, is to maintain the whole. To 'maintain' it is to keep it in 'equilibrium'. That is what mutual dependence means. The idea of equilibrium is not completely strange to historians either; in its eighteenth-century form, 'balance', it was an important part of the conceptual apparatus of Edward Gibbon. When he diagnosed the fall of the Roman Empire as the result of its 'immoderate greatness', he was thinking in terms of disequilibrium. But sociologists and anthropologists do more than use the imagery of structure and equilibrium. The questions they ask and the answers they give to these questions are – or were till comparatively recently – defined in these terms. For example, Malinowski, one of the pioneers of the functionalist approach, treated myths primarily if not exclusively as stories with social functions. A myth, Malinowski suggested, is a story about the past which serves, as he put it, as a 'charter'; that is, it performs the function of justifying some institution in the present and thus of keeping it in being. He was probably thinking not only of his Trobriand Islanders but also of Magna Carta (Malinowski, 1926).

One of the most brilliant discussions of these issues occurs in a book whose author deliberately avoids the terms 'structure' and 'function', a book written by a social anthropologist about tribal Africa but carrying much wider implications. Max Gluckman emphasises that the functional approach, far from stating the obvious, as one might have thought, is really paradoxical. The function of the feud, for example, is not to threaten the peace but to keep it, because his conflict of loyalties gives each individual an interest in the maintenance of social cohesion. Again, Gluckman argues that 'rebellions, so far from destroying the established social order, work so that they even support this order'; that is, their function is to maintain this order by acting as a safety valve. Again, discussing the Zulu rites of reversal, he makes the point that the annual lifting of the customary taboos 'serves to emphasise them' (Gluckman, 1955). In other words, the words a leading American sociologist, the 'latent' function of an institution may not be the same as its 'manifest' function (Merton, 1948).

There are obvious objections to this structural-functionalist approach, but before considering its weaknesses it is important to draw attention to its very real strengths. This approach does make it easier to understand how a social structure can persist while the individuals who at any point make it up are continually changing. It makes certain myths, beliefs and rituals more intelligible. Let us take a famous example from mediaeval history, that of the 'Donation of Constantine'; that is, the story that the emperor Constantine gave land to the papacy in return for being cured from leprosy by Pope Sylvester. The Donation of Constantine is a story which exemplifies Malinowski's interpretation of myth as 'charter'. The function of the story was to justify the existence of the Papal States, the temporal power of the papacy. For an example of the social function of beliefs, one might take witchcraft in Tudor and Stuart England. According to one recent historian of the subject, the belief in witchcraft served to maintain the traditional type of co-operation and charity between neighbours in English village communities because the richer neighbours feared being cursed or bewitched by the poorer ones if they turned them away from the door empty-handed (Thomas, 1971). As for ritual, two sociologists analysed the coronation of Queen Elizabeth II in terms of the social function of expressing and strengthening the moral consensus of British society (Shils and Young, 1953). It is not difficult to see how historians could analyse earlier coronations or other rituals in similar terms, and some have done so (Nelson, 1975).

At this point it may be useful to take a slightly more extended example of a functionalist approach to a past society, the Venetian Republic. In the sixteenth and seventeenth centuries, Venice was much admired by foreigners for the stability of its political and social system. The Venetians themselves explained their stability in terms of their 'mixed' or 'balanced' constitution, in which the doge provided the monarchical element, the Senate the aristocratic and the Great Council the democratic. In practice, however, the three elements were not balanced as evenly as all that. The doge had high status but little power. As one sixteenth-century Venetian put it, the doge was no more than a 'tavern sign'. The Great Council had more power, but it was not dominant. In practice Venice was ruled by an oligarchy of some 200 leading nobles, known as the *grandi*, who shared the key political offices between them. It might be said that the myth of noble democracy and equality, like the associated myth of the balanced constitution, functioned to keep the system as it was, inequalities and imbalances included.

There was always a danger of conflict between the *grandi* and the lesser nobles, but the conflict is only rarely visible in the documents. One of the rare occasions was in 1625, when the new doge, Zuan Corner, who favoured his close relations more than was customary, was opposed by Renier Zen, who made himself the spokesman of the lesser nobles. It was said that Zen wanted to have Corner deposed, and one of Corner's sons did try to assassinate this persistent critic. However, Zen was brought into the ruling oligarchy, Corner died, the conflict was defused and a compromise achieved. How was this managed? A possible answer to this question is to echo Gluckman's explanation of 'the peace in the feud', and to suggest that in Venice, too, conflicting allegiances served the function of social cohesion. The lesser nobles were pulled one way by group solidarity and hostility to the greater nobles, but they were tugged in the opposite direction by the ties of patronage which bound them as individuals to individual *grandi* (cf. p.72f below). Caught in this conflict, they had a stake in compromise.

The most articulate group of commoners who might have challenged the Venetian oligarchy were the citizens, a relatively small group of some 2,000 to 3,000 adult males. They enjoyed certain privileges to compensate for their exclusion from the Great Council. Certain offices in the administration were reserved for them; their daughters not infrequently married nobles; certain religious fraternities associated nobles with citizens. It might be said that these privileges had the function of making citizens feel that they mattered to the nobles and so of detaching them from the other commoners.

We have still to consider the majority of the population

of Venice, about 150,000 people. Some contemporaries explained the absence of conflict between the nobles and other Venetians in terms of cheap corn, which was subsidised by the government in order to keep the people quiet. Man does not live by bread alone, but the Venetian government offered 'circuses' as well; that is, splendid public rituals. These rituals included the Wedding of the Sea on Ascension Day and also Carnival, a ritual of reversal in which the authorities could be criticised with impunity, a safety valve like the Zulu rituals described by Gluckman. Again, the fishermen of Venice were allowed to elect their own doge, who was solemnly received and kissed by the real doge, a ritual with the function of persuading ordinary people that they participated in a political system from which they were in fact effectively excluded (Burke, 1974).

This example has been discussed at length in the belief that the linked concepts of structure and function are of use to historians as well as to their neighbours in sociology and social anthropology. However, there are dangers in using these concepts and the associated ideas of 'consensus', 'cohesion', 'equilibrium' and 'integration'.

One might begin with the obvious historians' objection – though it is difficult to raise a serious objection to sociological methods which has not been anticipated by sociologists themselves. This objection may be phrased as a brutally short question. Where have the people gone? Where do contemporaries and their intentions fit in? Or, as a sociologist might put it: what about the actors and their definition of the situation? On this problem, two comments.

The first point is that contemporaries may see what is going on. What looks like a 'latent' function may in fact be 'manifest' to some people. Some seventeenth-century Italians, for example, were well aware of the devices by which the Venetian oligarchy maintained itself in power. Without their recorded comments, a functional analysis of the Venetian system would have been much more difficult. Again, the safety valve theory of ritualised rebellion was no invention of modern anthropologists, despite the steam technology of the metaphor. Richard Lassels, an English observer of a seventeenth-century Roman carnival, declared that 'all this is allowed the Italians that they may give a little vent to their spirits which have been stifled in for a whole year and are ready else to choke with gravity and melancholy'.

However, it does not really matter, so far as the validity of this type of explanation is concerned, whether or not contemporaries were aware of the social functions of their customs and institutions. They had their motives for action, which the historian must take into account if he is giving a narrative of events over the short term; but to see how the social structure persists over the long term, it is necessary to have recourse to functional explanations. As a sociologist might say, explanations in terms of individual motives may work perfectly well at the micro-level, the level of face-to-face interaction, but they do not explain what happens at the macro-level, the level of the whole society. To speak in terms of social functions is to run the risk of reifying or personifying this 'society', but the danger can be avoided. The metaphor is a useful piece of shorthand for what cannot be explained in terms of individuals and their intentions (cf. Bendix, 1967).

A more telling objection to the functionalist approach than asking where the people have gone is to point out that it assumes a social or moral consensus which is in practice extremely questionable. To return for a moment to the coronation of Queen Elizabeth II: it has been interpreted as a ritual affirming a consensus and so functioning to maintain the social structure, to integrate society, to preserve cohesion and equilibrium (Shils and Young, 1953). But did the different social groups in Britain in the 1950s really share the same basic values? It has been argued that they did not, and this argument generates a different interpretation of the coronation as an anachronistic ritual which was not taken seriously by many people (Birnbaum, 1955). Similar questions could be raised about the consensus, or lack of consensus, in seventeenth-century Venice and the function of the Wedding of the Sea. Questions like these

would obviously have to be raised afresh in each new situation. All that can be said here is that it must not be assumed
that the values of the ruling class are shared by other
groups. However, the sharing is possible. Alternatively, the
different groups participating in the ritual might interpret it
in different ways. Ritual might not so much affirm a
consensus as serve to create one. The process might be
interpreted by a cynic, as non-Venetians tended to interpret
Venetian rituals, as a cunning attempt by the ruling elite to
manipulate the rest by means of the myth of consensus.
However, the process would work irrespective of whether
the elite was conscious of it or not.

Another objection to the functionalist approach centres
on the notion of equilibrium and the problem of change.
'Social equilibrium' is of course a mechanical metaphor,
and one which appealed particularly to the sociologist
Vilfredo Pareto, perhaps because he was trained as an
engineer. Like 'society', it is a term which lends itself to
reification. The notion has also been criticised as too static.
'Real societies can never be in equilibrium' (Leach, 1954,
introduction). In a recent study of the English Revolution,
Lawrence Stone suggested that in England between 1529
and 1629, economic growth and social change led to 'disequilibrium' between the political and social systems, and
that measures designed to restore this equilibrium in fact
upset it still further. The reaction of one reviewer was to
ask 'When was there an equilibrium?', and to conclude
that the concept was 'misleading when applied to late
mediaeval and early modern Europe' (Stone, 1972;
Koenigsberger, 1974).

All these criticisms are a little exaggerated. Pareto, to
return to him, did not see societies in terms of a 'perfect' or
static equilibrium, but rather in terms of a 'dynamic' equilibrium, defined as 'such a state that if it is artificially sub-
jected to some modification...a reaction at once takes
place, tending to restore it to its real, its normal state'
(Pareto, 1916, section 2068). Equilibrium should not in any
case be equated with lack of disturbance, with peace, but
simply with the maintenance of the social structure. To

Koenigsberger's question, 'When was there an equilibrium?', one might answer 'in fifteenth-century England'. Despite the Wars of the Roses, there was no major change in the social structure at this time (cf. Lander, 1969). Similarly in Venice in the sixteenth and seventeenth centuries there were external wars and internal conflicts, but the society and the state remained in relative equilibrium.

Irrespective of the possible dangers of the term 'equilibrium', functional analysis has often been criticised as too static. To focus on what serves to maintain the social structure is to neglect change. This is a fair criticism of the functionalist approach as it has usually (but not always) been practised, but there is no reason why historians or sociologists should not study beliefs, institutions or groups which serve to undermine a given social structure and to promote change. It is possible to discover myths which justify change as well as myths which justify the *status quo*. An obvious historical example is the 'myth of Magna Carta', as it is sometimes called. This record öf the concessions which King John made to his barons was interpreted in very different ways by later generations, notably in the seventeenth century, and these interpretations served a social function, that of justifying or 'legitimating' change by making it appear to be founded on precedent, on tradition. Again, the belief in witchcraft in Tudor and Stuart England has been described as 'a means of effecting a deep social change', the change from a neighbourly village community to a more individualistic society. Some of the richer villagers justified their refusal of charity to poor old women by describing these women as witches (Macfarlane, 1970, ch. 15; contrast p. 44, above).

To sum up. The concept 'function' is a useful item in the historian's tool kit, provided that it is not blunted by indiscriminate use. It carries with it temptations to neglect social change, social conflict and individual motives, but all these temptations can be avoided. There is no need to assume that every institution in a given society has a positive function, without any costs (or 'dysfunctions'). There is no need to assume that a given institution is indispensable to the performance of a given function, for different institutions may act as functional 'equivalents' (Merton, 1948). In Britain today, for example, schools perform some functions which were once exercised by the family. There is no need to forget that society is composed of individuals with intentions. The assumption of the functionalist approach is that a society cannot be understood simply by investigating the intentions of its members, because of the importance of unintended consequences; and that these unintended consequences are structured, that they can be better understood if society were regarded as if it were a machine in equilibrium. However, functional explanations should not be seen as replacements for other kinds of historical explanation, which they complement rather than contradict, since they tend to be answers to different questions rather than different answers to the same questions (cf. Gellner, 1958). The suggestion is not that we throw overboard traditional historical explanations, but rather that we take on board something useful for which historians have in fact no functional equivalent.

SOCIAL ROLE

Another concept central to sociology is that of social role, defined in terms of the pattern or 'norms' of behaviour associated with a particular status or position in the social structure: 'king', 'child', 'artist', or whatever. The metaphor of the world as a stage goes back to ancient Greece, but it has been developed and made more precise in sociological theory, notably, in the last twenty years, by Erving Goffman, who has linked it to concepts such as 'performance' and 'personal space' in order to elucidate what he calls 'impression management' or 'the presentation of self' (Goffman, 1958). One way of defining a role is in terms of the behaviour expected of its holder. 'Child', for example, is a social role which may be defined by the expectations of adults, expectations which have changed a good deal in Western Europe since the Middle Ages. The 7-year-old, who had reached the 'age of reason', as it was called, was once expected to behave as much like an adult as possible. He or she was regarded as a small, weak, inefficient, inexperienced and ignorant adult, but an adult all the same (Ariès, 1960). Roles may be defined in terms of the expectations of other people, provided that it is remembered that different people may have incompatible expectations of the same role, leading to what sociologists call 'role strain' in anyone who occupies this position.

It could be argued that historians have much to gain from making a greater and a more systematic use of the concept 'role' than they have so far done. Doing this would encourage them to explain in structural terms behaviour which has been discussed in terms of personalities and often condemned rather too easily and ethnocentrically. Royal favourites, for example, have often been misunderstood in this way, as if a favourite was simply a bad man who happened to coincide with a weak king and corrupted him. In fact, 'favourite' was a social role with definite functions in that microcosm of the social system, the court. Kings, like other people, needed friends; and, unlike other people, they needed unofficial advisers. They needed, on occasion, a means of bypassing the formal machinery of their own government. They needed someone they could trust, someone who would have to be faithful to them because his own position depended on this, someone who was independent of the great nobles who surrounded the king. A favourite was all these things. Specific favourites, like Piers Gaveston in the reign of Edward II or the Duke of Buckingham in the reign of James I, may have been disasters, but there was a hole of this shape in the court system which needed to be filled, and a pattern of behaviour associated with this particular status. Like the power of eunuchs in the Byzantine and Chinese empires, the power of favourites cannot be explained in terms of the weakness of a particular monarch (on eunuch power, see Hopkins, 1978, pp. 172 – 96).

Some historical monographs do make good use of the concept of role. T. C. Cochran, for example, has discussed the 'executive role' in nineteenth-century America and the pressures which shaped it. Peter Lloyd, a social anthropologist, has written about role strain in the case of the *oba*, the sacred ruler of the traditional Yoruba kingdoms. The *oba* was surrounded by chiefs who expected him both to assert himself and to accept their decisions (Cochran, 1953, ch. 16; Lloyd, 1968). Lloyd's argument has obvious relevance to the history of mediaeval and early modern Europe, where kings were in a sense sacred, and surrounded by barons who expected them to be both strong and docile. There was nothing a king could do which would satisfy these contradictory expectations. Reverence for the role of sacred king might inhibit open criticism of its holder, since it was held that 'the king can do no wrong'; it did not inhibit attacks on his policies by other means, notably the denunciation of his 'evil councillors'. This was at once an indirect way of criticising the king and a direct expression of noble hatred for rivals who were not great nobles but 'raised from the dust' by the king's favour. The continuity of such criticisms, made, for example, by the chronicler Ordericus Vitalis against Henry I of England in the twelfth century and by the memoir-writer Saint-Simon against Louis XIV of France in the seventeenth century, suggests that the problem was a structural one, despite the fact that contemporaries continued to see it in personal terms (cf. Rosenthal, 1967). Kings were not, incidentally, the only victims of inconsistent expectations about roles in mediaeval politics. Kings often expected their barons to be strong and weak at once, efficient enforcers of the peace in their own territories yet not 'overmighty subjects' (Lander, 1969, ch. 7).

It would be misleading to suggest that contemporaries were completely unaware of the idea of 'role'. Shakespeare was not the only dramatist of early modern times to tell his audience that 'each man in his life plays many parts'. The author of *The Courtier*, who explains how much hard work has to go into the production of apparently natural and spontaneous behaviour, aristocratic as to the manner born, would not have had too much to learn from the author of *The Presentation of Self in Everyday Life* (Castiglione, 1528; Goffman, 1958).

However, the systematic use of the concept 'role' by historians of early modern Europe (say) might reveal to them neglected features of the culture and society of the time, or at least warn them against interpreting certain artefacts too simply. Portraits, for example, reveal what the artist considered (or what he thought his client considered) the pose, gestures, expression and 'properties' appropriate to a particular social role, including armour for nobles who never fought and books for bishops who never studied. To play the great nobleman in England in the sixteenth and seventeenth centuries involved vast expenditure on properties of this kind, including magnificent clothes and a great house, without which the occupant of this role might not have received the respect or 'worship' he considered his due. Lawrence Stone's vivid and penetrating description of 'conspicuous consumption' by the English peerage on clothes and houses, hospitality and funerals, owes not a little, as he would be the first to admit, to that early classic of sociology, *The Theory of the Leisure Class* (Veblen, 1899; Stone, 1965).

It should be added that a given social group may play different roles at different periods, and that at a given moment its members may have a choice of roles. The role of 'king', for example, did not entail the same expectations in England in 1760 as it had done in 1066. It might be possible to write the social history of the artist, in Italy, for example, in terms of different roles which were dominant in chronological order, though at any given time there was usually more than one available to artists who could adapt their behaviour to the pattern required. Thus the dominant role for artists in mediaeval Italy was 'craftsman'. At the Renaissance the leading role was 'courtier', a role played with distinction by Giotto, for example, and above all by Raphael. Since the middle of the nineteenth century, a new role has become available, that of 'rebel' (cf. Bell, 1961).

KINSHIP AND FAMILY

The most obvious example of an institution composed of a

set of mutually dependent roles is the family. In the last few years, the history of the family has become one of the most rapidly growing fields of historical research, and in the course of cultivating this field, historians have found themselves obliged to learn something of the language of demography, sociology and social anthropology. To discuss changes in the structure of the family presupposes some kind of typology or classification.

The best-known classification of family structures goes back more than a century to the Frenchman Frédéric Le Play, who distinguished three main types. There was the 'patriarchal', now called the 'joint' family, where the married sons remain under their father's roof; the 'stem family' (*famille souche*), in which only one married son remains; and finally the 'unstable', now known as the 'nuclear' or 'conjugal' family, which all the children leave on marriage (Le Play, 1871).

Unfortunately, there is disagreement over the definition of these three types of family structure. One way to define them is in terms of the size and composition of the household, which can often be discovered by analysing census data and other official sources. This is the approach associated with the Cambridge Group for the History of Population and Social Structure, and in particular with Peter Laslett, who distinguishes three main types of household. There is the 'simple family household', consisting of a 'conjugal family unit' such as a married couple or a widow and her children; the 'extended family household' (a conjugal family unit 'with the addition of one or more relatives other than offspring'); and finally, the 'multiple family household', including 'two or more conjugal family units connected by kinship or by marriage' (Laslett, 1972).

The household approach is beautifully precise, but it has its dangers for all that. In the first place, the differences between the households described as 'multiple', 'extended', or 'simple' may represent no more than phases in the developmental cycle of the same domestic group, which expands while the young couple are having children and contracts again as the children marry and move out.

This point, first made by the social anthropologists, has been illustrated vividly in a study of the peasant family in eighteenth-century Austria (Goody, 1958; Berkner, 1972).

A second objection to the treatment of household size and composition as an index of family structure brings us back once again to the question of the relation between hard and soft data. What the historian, like the sociologist, is trying to discover is the way in which family relationships are structured. However, this structure may not be revealed by the size of the household. The family is not just a residential unit. It is also, or may be on occasion, an economic or a legal unit. A group of relatives may own and exploit property in common. The family is also, obviously, a group with which its members identify, with which they are emotionally involved. This multiplicity of function poses problems for historians and sociologists alike. The economic, legal, residential and emotional units clearly overlap but they need not coincide. Hence an index based on co-residence may not tell historians what they most need to know about family structure in a given place and time. For example, relatives who live in separate households may live near one another and see one another virtually every day, a situation to which attention was drawn in a study of the working class in East London (Young and Willmott, 1957). Here a 'conjugal' household coexists with an 'extended' mentality, at least as far as the wife's relationship with her mother is concerned. There is something of a parallel to this situation in fifteenth-century Italy, at least among the patricians. In Florence, for example, noble kinsmen often lived in neighbouring palaces, met regularly in the family *loggia*, acted as an economic community and collaborated closely in political affairs. The history of the patrician family in Florence (or Venice, or Genoa, for that matter) cannot be written in terms of the household alone (Heers, 1974; Kent, 1977).

SOCIALISATION, DEVIANCE AND SOCIAL CONTROL

One of the most important of the family's functions is 'socialisation', defined as the process by which the social heritage, and in particular a society's 'norms', or rules of behaviour, are transmitted from one generation to the next. Since historians have long been aware of the importance of the transmission of cultural traditions, it may well be asked whether they have any particular need for the concept of 'socialisation'. One advantage of the concept is to serve as a reminder that a history of education should not limit itself to the instruction which takes place in specialist institutions such as schools (cf. Bailyn, 1960). Political attitudes, for example, may not be taught formally in schools but they often seem to be acquired early, so that it is useful to follow the lead of political scientists, as some historians have already done, and investigate modes of 'political socialisation' in the past. In seventeenth-century England, for example, the fact that children grew up in patriarchally ruled families must have made it easier for them to accept without questioning a patriarchally ruled society (Schochet, 1975). The employment of the term 'socialisation' might also suggest to historians that if they want to explain why a particular society had a particular system of formal education, it will be useful to look at the whole system of roles and norms, for a social system would not persist unless there was some kind of 'fit' between the norms transmitted by socialisation and the roles available for adults.

The problem is that to discuss socialisation into the norms of 'society' is to assume a consensus which is often questionable, as we have seen. Hence there is a place for another sociological approach to the transmission of norms, one which places more emphasis on conflict, class and compulsion, as Pierre Bourdieu and his collaborators do. Among Bourdieu's central concepts are 'cultural reproduction', 'habitus' and 'symbolic violence'. By 'cultural reproduction' is meant the tendency of society in general and the educational system in particular to reproduce itself by inculcating in the rising generation the values of the generation before. Traditions do not persist automatically, out of 'inertia', as historians sometimes put it. They are the result of a good deal of hard work by parents, teachers, priests, employers and other agents of socialisation. The concept 'cultural reproduction' draws attention to the effort involved in running on the spot, in keeping a given society more or less as it is. Bourdieu's second concept refers to what the rising generation are taught. He rejects the concept 'rules' as too mechanical, too inflexible to describe what is learned, and defines his alternative concept, 'habitus', as 'schemes enabling agents to generate an infinity of practices adapted to endlessly changing situations'. His third concept, 'symbolic violence', refers to the imposition of the culture (norms, values, habitus) of the ruling class on members of dominated groups, and especially to the process by which these dominated groups are made to recognise the ruling culture as legitimate and their own culture as illegitimate (Bourdieu, 1972; Bourdieu and Passeron, 1977).

It would be fascinating to have a history of the French or British educational system or, better, training system, written in these terms. When such a history has been written it will be easier to judge the strengths and weaknesses of the Bourdieu approach. The same goes for Basil Bernstein's stimulating and controversial discussion of socialisation into 'elaborated' and 'restricted' speech codes (Bernstein, 1970). However, retrospective socio-linguistics has scarcely begun. The nearest thing we have to a discussion of 'symbolic violence' in the past is perhaps the recent work on sixteenth-century attacks on popular religion by the Counter-Reformation clergy, and the process by which the peasants were persuaded to see their traditional culture as 'superstitious' and 'idolatrous', even 'diabolical', and to change their norms (Delumeau, 1971; Muchembled, 1978).

Of course, the norms are not always observed. 'Deviance', the sociological term for behaviour which violates the norms of a given social system, has the advantage of making it easier to understand hostile attitudes to groups as different in other respects as the insane, criminals, missionaries and revolutionaries. 'Deviance' implies a consensus which some people deviate from, but the term does not stand or fall with the acceptance of a consensus view as opposed to a conflict view of society. It has been suggested that 'social groups create deviance by making the rules whose infraction constitutes deviance and by applying those rules to particular people and labelling them as outsiders' (Becker, 1963). The moral would seem to be that deviance should be seen in terms of a clash between two social groups with different interests and values, the labellers (who have power) and the labelled (who do not).

This 'labelling' theory would seem to offer another useful perspective on witchcraft, discussed above (pp. 44, 49) in terms of 'function'. There seems little doubt that the authorities, in particular the inquisitors, created witchcraft in the later Middle Ages by describing wise women and other people as heretics and making them confess to being in league with the devil. This is not to say that no one in this period ever tried to harm anyone else by supernatural means, but only that *maleficia* of this kind were only one element in the stereotype of the witch (Cohn, 1975).

The advantage of discussing the witch hunts of the sixteenth and seventeenth centuries in terms of the labelling of deviants is that it encourages historians to ask who is labelling whom and why. In a similar way, it seems useful to study the problem of the so-called 'sturdy beggars' of Elizabethan England in terms of the labellers as well as the labelled, and to ask why it was that the ruling class saw able-bodied vagrants, who would later be described as 'unemployed', as nothing but idlers. Again, in his celebrated book on the history of madness, Michel Foucault has studied insanity from a similar point of view. He interprets what he calls the 'Great Confinement', the foundation in Paris in 1656 of the Hôpital Général for the poor and the insane, followed by the foundation of similar hospitals in the provinces, as 'an instance of order, of the monarchical and bourgeois order being organised in France during this period', the early years of Louis XIV (Foucault, 1961).

The idea that the authorities create deviance is one shocking sociological idea which may be of use to historians. Another is the suggestion that 'Some social structures exert a definite pressure upon certain persons in the society to engage in non-conformist rather than conformist conduct' (Merton, 1949). We have learned that in the Mediterranean world in the late sixteenth century banditry was rife and that the bandits included a substantial number of noblemen (Braudel, 1949, pp. 743 – 54). In this part of the world in this period, noblemen could not work without loss of honour. To beg they were likewise ashamed. An impoverished noble had therefore no alternative to starvation except robbery. He was in this sense socialised into deviance. The paradox reminds us of the danger of assuming that the norms of a given society are completely consistent.

All the same, deviance is punished and conformity rewarded, a process which sociologists often call 'social control', meaning the control which 'society' exercises over individuals. The concept 'social control' is not unlike that of 'public opinion', with which historians have long been familiar. It may be defined in terms of consensus and equilibrium. Social control is the enforcement of the consensus over norms, and the mechanism for the re-establishment of the social equilibrium which the deviants threaten. The question this language begs is, of course, who is 'society'? Who, for that matter, is 'the public'? If a given society is united and harmonious, this language may well be useful; if, on the other hand, a society is composed of social groups in conflict, each group with its own values, the term 'social control' is bound to mislead.

Where the term seems most useful is in the analysis of face-to-face situations where the non-conformist confronts the community, as in the cases, classics in sociology, of the rate-buster in the factory or the private who sucks up to the officers (Roethlisberger and Dickson, 1941; Stouffer *et al.*, 1949). For a historian of pre-industrial Europe, one of the most striking forms of social control is the charivari. The old man who married a young girl, or the husband who allowed himself to be beaten by his wife, had transgressed the norms of the community and was punished by the maskers in the name of the community (Davis, 1971; Thompson, 1972). Even here it is not altogether clear who 'the community' are; everyone in the village, or just the young men who organised the charivari? Were the older men or the women likely to see the situation in the same light?

A recent study of confession in the fifteenth century described it as 'an instrument of social control' (Tentler, 1974). This is a little dangerous. If the laity defined deviance ('sin') in the same way as the clergy, well and good; but we cannot be sure that this was the case in the fifteenth century. To describe confession as an instrument of 'symbolic violence' would make the opposite assumption, and would be equally dangerous, given the state of the evidence. It is more dangerous still to discuss the relationship between an eighteenth-century English squire and his tenants in terms of social control, when the squire was not enforcing the norms of the village community (indeed, by punishing poachers, he might be transgressing those norms), but rather exercising power in his own interests or at best enforcing a rival set of norms, the norms of the central government and his own class (Perkin, 1969, pp. 32f.; contrast E. P. Thompson, 1975, and cf. Donajgrodzki, 1977).

'Class', however, raises some of the most acute conceptual problems in the whole of social history and sociology.

SOCIAL CLASS AND SOCIAL STRATIFICATION

Social stratification is an area where historians are especially liable to use technical terms such as 'caste', 'mobility', and so on, without being aware of all the problems involved and the distinctions which sociologists have found it useful to draw. The concept 'class' in particular is as ambiguous as it is indispensable. In most if not all societies there are inequalities in the distribution of wealth and other advantages such as status and power. However, it is often difficult to identify the principles governing this distribution or to describe the social relationships to which these inequalities give rise. These relationships include the sense of solidarity within a given group, its sense of difference from (and possibly conflict with) other groups, and the sense of hierarchy, of position relative to others. To describe relationships such as these it seems impossible to escape from metaphor, whether we talk about the social 'ladder' or 'pyramid' or prefer the geological image of social 'stratification'.

A historian may well ask what is wrong with accepting the actors' image of a given social structure rather than imposing a modern one, since contemporaries knew their society from within. The inhabitants of a seventeenth-century French village doubtless understood that society better than we can ever do. But what of their view of their province, or of France as a whole? Historians today, with their access to official documents and their quantitative methods, are in some respects better informed than contemporaries about the distribution of wealth and other advantages in seventeenth-century France.

Another reason for not adopting contemporary views of a given society is that they often contradict one another. The pyramid looks different according to one's place in it, and some contemporary statements about the social structure should be taken as justifications rather than detached descriptions. The traditional mediaeval view of society was one of the mutual dependence of three groups: the clergy, the knights and the peasants. However, this division of society into 'those who pray, those who fight and those who work' looks extremely like a justification of those who do not work by those who do not work. Contemporary views, although an indispensable part of the data to be analysed, are unlikely to make the most appropriate framework for that analysis.

In this area it is even more difficult than elsewhere in social history to do without a model (Ossowski, 1957, ch. 9; Stone, 1966). The best-known model is, of course, that of Marx, despite the fact that his chapter on 'class' in *Capital* consists of no more than a few lines, followed by the note 'here the manuscript breaks off'. Marx's other writings allow the missing chapter to be fitted together like a jig-saw (Bendix and Lipset, 1953; Dahrendorf, 1957, pp. 9 – 18).

For Marx, a class is a social group with a particular func-tion in the process of production. Owners of land, owners of capital and workers who own nothing but their hands are the three great social classes, corresponding to the three factors of production in classical economics, land, labour and capital. The different functions of these classes give them conflicting interests and make them likely to think and act in different ways. Hence history is the story of class conflict.

The criticism most frequently levelled against this model is also the most unfair: that it simplifies. It is the function of a model to simplify in order to make the real world more intelligible (see above, p. 35). The social historian of nineteenth-century Britain, say, working from official documents like the census, finds that the population is described by a bewildering number of occupational cate-gories. To make more general statements about British society it is necessary to collapse these categories into broader ones. Marx offers the social historian some broad categories together with an explanation of his choice. In this sense he provides social history with just the 'back-bone' it has always needed. He emphasises differences between his three groups at the expense of differences within them, and he omits marginal cases, like that of the self-employed man, who does not fit into any of his three categories; but after all, one expects such simplifications from a model.

It is more worrying that Marx's model is not quite as clear and simple as it looks. He uses the term 'class' in several different senses. Sometimes he distinguishes three classes, the owners of land, capital and labour; sometimes he distinguishes only two, exploiters and exploited, oppres-sors and oppressed. At times he makes use of a broad definition of class, at others of a narrower one. According to the broad definition, Roman slaves and plebeians, mediaeval serfs and journeymen were all classes (or rather part of the same working class), because their interests were in conflict with those of their lords and masters. According to the narrow definition, the French peasants were not a class in 1850 because they lacked class-consciousness, in other words a sense of solidarity with one another across regional boundaries. They were not a community according to Marx but an aggregate of similar but distinct people, like 'a sack of potatoes'.

It is scarcely surprising to find that it is historians of Europe in the nineteenth century, and more particularly of England, the society where Marx was writing and where the language of class was coming into use, who have found his model most useful (E. P. Thompson, 1963; Perkin, 1969). For other kinds of society, other models may be more appropriate, models which do not distinguish social groups on the basis of their position in the production process but according to other criteria. For India, for example, the obvious model is that of 'caste', defined as a stratification system in which the basic principle is the opposition between the 'pure' and the 'impure'. For pre-industrial Europe, there would be a good case for choosing the model of 'estate' or 'status group' as defined by Max Weber.

Weber distinguished 'classes', defined as groups of people whose opportunities in life (*Lebenschancen*) were determined by the market situation, from 'estates' (*Stände*), whose fate was determined by the status or honour (*ständische Ehre*) accorded them. The status of the latter groups was acquired by birth, defined legally and might carry power and privilege with it. High status was marked by what the American sociologist Thorstein Veblen had called 'conspicuous consumption' (Veblen, 1899). Where Marx defined his classes in terms of production, Weber defined his estates in terms of consumption. In this sense the American sociologist who devised the 'living room scale' to measure status (see above, p. 39) was in the Weber tradition. However, for Weber consumption patterns are not always reliable indices of status. He was aware of possible discrepancies in the distribution of different kinds of advantage. In the long run, he suggested, property confers status, but in the short run 'both propertied and propertyless people can belong to the same *Stand*' (Weber, 1921).

Weber's model was put forward as an alternative to that of Marx, and Marxists have in their turn answered Weber, pointing out, for example, that values like 'status' are not the expression of a consensus in a given society so much as values imposed by the dominant class on everyone else (Parkin, 1971, pp. 40 – 7). The debate is complicated by the fact that the two men had different interests and were trying to answer different questions about inequality. Marx was especially concerned with dominance and conflict, while Weber was interested in values and in life-styles. Consequently, the class and estate models, like the conflict and consensus models, may be seen as complementary rather than contradictory ways of looking at society, each of them revealing some of its features at the price of obscuring others (Ossowski, 1957, ch. 12).

This point about complementarity may be illustrated by examining the use which has been made of the rival models in the analysis of one pre-industrial society, France in the seventeenth and eighteenth centuries. Shortly after the Second World War, a Soviet historian, Boris Porshnev, published a book on popular revolts between 1623 and 1648 which analysed French society in class terms, emphasising the conflicts between landlords and tenants, masters and journeymen, rulers and ruled (Porshnev, 1948).

This Marxist analysis was firmly rejected by a French historian, Roland Mousnier, who suggested that it should be replaced by a model of the French social structure reminiscent of Weber's status groups. Mousnier argued, and still argues, that the fundamental divisions in French society in the seventeenth century were those between the clergy, the nobles and the rest; that is, between the three 'estates' or 'orders'. He accused Porshnev of anachronism for using the term 'class' in a seventeenth-century context. Mousnier accepted contemporary views of French society, assuming a consensus between them. He relied in particular on a treatise on 'orders' and 'dignities' by the lawyer Charles Loyseau, a treatise which Porshnev had discussed as an attempt by an ennobled bourgeois to justify the social claims of the group to which he belonged. Where Porshnev used the term 'bourgeoisie' more or less as Marx defined it (allowing for the fact that the seventeenth-century bourgeoisie invested their capital in land and in 'offices' like magistracies rather than in industry), Mousnier discussed how the term 'bourgeois' was used in the period itself. Like Weber, he drew attention to the fact that wealth did not altogether determine status, so that a poor noble was higher in the social hierarchy than a rich merchant. He suggested that 'vertical solidarity' between landlord and tenant or patron and client was stronger at this period than 'horizontal solidarity' between equals (Mousnier, 1969).

With these different models of the social structure go divergent analyses of the popular revolts in seventeenth-century France. Porshnev sees the rebels as men with a conscious aim, to overthrow the ruling class and end the 'feudal' regime which was oppressing them. Mousnier, on the other hand, sees the revolts as blind 'furies' without a coherent programme. Porshnev believes that in each region the peasants co-operated against noble landlords, burning down their châteaux, while Mousnier believes that in each locality landlords and peasants collaborated against the central government, joining forces to ambush the tax collectors. Each historian can produce instances which fit his interpretation, but the evidence is too fragmentary to determine which instances were the more typical. Since the revolts do not cast enough light on the social structure, we are forced to return to the social structure to illuminate the revolts.

Neither legal treatises on the three estates of the realm nor official reports to the central government about popular disturbances are ideal evidence for the nature of a social structure. Roughly speaking, these sources correspond respectively to what sociologists call the 'self-rating' and the 'reputational' approaches, where interviewers or questionnaires invite respondents to indicate either their own position in the social hierarchy or that of other people. Sources of this kind need to be supplemented by what sociologists call the 'objective approach', the study of what people do rather than of what they say, and especially the study of who marries whom, since intermarriage would seem to be a good indicator of social equality.

This third approach has also been practised by historians of the old regime in France. For example, a study of all the surviving marriage contracts recorded by Paris notaries in the year 1749 (2,597 contracts, to be exact), was made in order to determine the socio-professional hierarchy in Paris at this time. Thirteen social categories ranging from journeyman to nobleman were established on the basis of three criteria, occupation, fortune and marriage (Daumard and Furet, 1961). This study was also attacked by Mousnier, who accused the authors of anachronism for their stress on the connections between the economic and the social hier-archies, and also for borrowing their socio-professional categories from mid-twentieth-century surveys by the INS, the Institut National des Statistiques (Mousnier, 1964). A somewhat different quantitative study of social structure has since been carried out by one of Mousnier's pupils. It concerns the little town of Châteaudun between 1525 and 1789. Like the Daumard-Furet study it is computer-based and relies on the evidence of marriages to establish who regarded whom as social equals. However, its four basic social categories are deliberately vaguer than the thirteen categories of Daumard and Furet. They consist of the clergy, higher groups (*groupes supérieures*), craftsmen and shopkeepers, and lower strata (*basses couches*) (Couturier, 1969).

In England, as in France, historians of the seventeenth and eighteenth centuries have been grappling with the problem of conceptualising the social structure. Lawrence Stone has contrasted what he calls the 'United Nations' model of English society in 1500, with the aristocracy and gentry towering over everyone else, with the 'San Gimignano' model of England 200 years later, by which time different professions, such as the law, the church and medicine, had risen in status to rival the gentry (Stone, 1966). For the eighteenth century, the crucial problem is that of characterising the groups at the bottom of the social pyramid. Edward Thompson, who has turned his attention to the period before 'the making of the English working class', speaks of 'the plebs' in the eighteenth century in contrast to the 'working class' in the nineteenth. The plebs were not a class because they lacked class-consciousness. Vertical solidarity still outweighed horizontal solidarity. On the other hand, vertical solidarity was not so strong that the plebs did not revolt against the established order. There were revolts, but they took a different form from those of the nineteenth century. Thompson sums them up in the paradox of 'class struggle without class' (E. P. Thompson, 1963, 1978).

This brief summary of a controversial subject, the most conceptually complicated in social history, suggests two provisional conclusions. The first is Ossowski's point that rival models may both help in the analysis of the same society. The use of the INS categories to analyse Parisian society in 1749 has the advantage of permitting comparisons and contrasts with Paris 200 years later. On the other hand, an analysis in terms of eighteenth-century categories makes it easier to understand eighteenth-century behaviour. Again, the 'class' model and the 'estate' model each alert the user to some of the social relationships in seventeenth-century France at the price of hiding others. It is unlikely that Weber, who had drawn attention to instances of 'class action' in pre-industrial Europe, would have been surprised by this conclusion.

A second point is that although both models help us to understand both kinds of society, the estates model seems especially relevant to pre-industrial societies and the class model to industrial ones. Formal definitions of the social hierarchy carry more weight in the first case, informal definitions in the second. Class-consciousness is naturally encouraged by the growing interdependence of different regions in the capitalist economy (Hobsbawm, 1971a).

SOCIAL MOBILITY

Like 'class', 'social mobility' is a term familiar enough to historians, like J. A. Schumpeter's famous image of it: 'the upper strata of society are like hotels which are indeed always full of people, but people who are forever changing'. In recent years conferences and special issues of journals have been devoted to the theme of social mobility in history. However, there are distinctions to be drawn and pitfalls to be avoided. It seems useful to make three distinctions in particular. The first is that between mobility up the social ladder and mobility downwards, although studies of downward mobility are hard to find. The second distinction is between mobility within an individual lifetime ('intragenerational') and mobility spread over several generations ('intergenerational'). The third distinction is between individual mobility and group mobility, a distinction which sometimes failed to be drawn in the celebrated controversy of the 1950s over the so-called 'rise of the gentry' in England between 1540 and 1640. It is necessary to distinguish the rise of the gentry relative to other social groups from the rise of individuals out of the gentry and into the peerage, and from the rise of other individuals into the gentry. Group mobility in the strict sense involves a change in the social structure, the adding of some rooms to Schumpeter's hotel.

As a participant in one conference on social mobility pointed out, historians of all periods seem to resent the imputation that 'their' society is static, and insist on regarding it as 'fluid', 'open', or 'mobile'. Perhaps no stratified society has ever been in a state of zero mobility, which would mean that all children enjoyed (or suffered from) the same wealth, status and power as their parents. The crucial question to ask about social mobility in a given society is surely a relative one. Was the rate of mobility higher in seventeenth-century England (say) than in fifteenth-century England, seventeenth-century France, seventeenth-century Japan? A quantitative, comparative approach virtually imposes itself. In the case of twentieth-century industrial societies, such an approach has already been carried out, concluding that despite the American emphasis on equality of opportunity, there has been no less social mobility in Europe than in the United States (Lipset and Bendix, 1959). It would be fascinating to have a Lipset and Bendix for pre-industrial societies, if the pitfalls of comparison can be avoided.

One example of these pitfalls is provided by a study of China in the Ming and Ch'ing periods (1368 – 1911), which argued that Chinese was much more open than European society in the same period (Ping-Ti, 1958 – 9). The evidence for the high rate of social mobility in China was provided by the lists of successful candidates in the civil service examinations, lists which provided information about the social origins of candidates. However, as a critic was quick to point out, 'data on the social origins of a ruling class do not constitute data on overall amounts of mobility or on the life chances of lower-class persons'. Why not? Because the relative size of the elite, its proportion to the rest of the population, has also to be taken into account, and Chinese mandarins were, as elites go, a small group (Dibble, 1960 – 1).

Modes of social mobility are another fascinating topic in comparative history. The Chinese had their examination system, from the end of the sixth century to the beginning of the twentieth. In Western society, a stranger whose status was unknown would be asked who his father was, but in China he was asked how many examinations he had passed. The Ottoman Empire had its 'tribute of children', a system whereby the administrative and military elites were recruited from the Christian subject population. The recruits were selected on the basis of ability, streamed, given a thorough education and employed as officials or as soldiers. They were also converted to Islam, thus cutting them off from their cultural roots and making them more dependent on the sultan, but also ensuring that sons were not eligible to follow their fathers into office (Parry, 1969). As for pre-industrial Europe, it had the church, for a career open to talent was easier to make in black than in scarlet. English examples include William of Wykeham, Bishop of Winchester, whose motto was 'Manners' (not birth) 'makyth man'; Thomas Cranmer, a yeoman's son who became Archbishop of Canterbury; William Laud, the son of a Reading clothier, another Archbishop of Canterbury; and Richard Neile, the son of a tallow chandler, Bishop of Durham, which was (like Winchester) one of the richest sees in England. It would be interesting to have a comparative study of the varying opportunities for social mobility afforded by the church in different regions and in different periods. Another well-known avenue of social mobility in pre-industrial Europe was the law. Its importance has been noted in fifteenth-century England, in sixteenth-century Germany, in seventeenth-century France. All over Europe, lawyers were in demand in the sixteenth and seventeenth centuries to fill posts in the growing state bureaucracy. Ambitious fathers put their sons to study law so that they would rise in the world, whether in private practice or in government service. This is what Petrarch's father intended, and Luther's, and Calvin's, though all three parents were disappointed. Less orthodox routes to the top must not be forgotten. Crime has been studied by a sociologist as a means of social mobility for social groups excluded from other avenues to success, groups such as the Irish and the Italians in the United States in the early twentieth century (Bell, 1953).

BUREAUCRACY

Political historians, generalising about institutional changes in one or more states at a given period, have coined such phrases as 'the state as a work of art', the 'new monarchies', the 'Tudor revolution in government', the rise of 'absolutism', the 'nineteenth-century revolution in government', and so on. To a sociologist all these changes will look like local examples of stages of transition from one major type of government to another, from what Max Weber called a 'patrimonial' to what he called a 'bureaucratic' system. Weber's typology is one of the most important contributions to the theory of political organisation since the Greeks distinguished monarchy, aristocracy and democracy. Weber defined bureaucratic government as an impersonal system with a sharp distinction between the public and the private sphere. A bureaucratic system is one administered by full-time officials appointed by formal procedures (such as examinations), specially trained for the job, organised in a formal hierarchy, using written records, and operating with fixed areas of jurisdiction. The patrimonial system may be defined as the reverse of all this, with part-time officials, informal organisation, oral commands, overlapping jurisdictions, and little distinction between the public and the private. Weber thought of the bureaucratic system as 'rational', as opposed to 'traditional', and he believed that the process of bureaucratisation was one of the major trends in the history of the West – like capitalism, to which it was connected (Weber, 1920 – 1).

It will be obvious that the administrative reforms of nineteenth-century Britain, like the opening of the civil service to competition, and the abolition of patronage, involve a move towards what Weber called the 'bureaucratic' model. Under the influence of Weber, some administrative historians have recently been asking more sociological questions, historians of Prussia in particular, appropriately enough, since the Prussian system, like the Chinese, was one of the most famous bureaucracies in the world and no doubt played its part in inspiring Weber's typology in the first place. Thus a recent study of the Prussian bureaucracy 'in crisis' in the mid-nineteenth century adopts a Weberian approach, focusing on patterns of recruitment and training and the development of 'increasingly rational and functional patterns of thought', and relating the modernisation of the Prussian bureaucracy to the industrialisation and urbanisation which were taking place in Germany at the same time (Gillis, 1971).

Weber's questions have also been asked about administration in pre-industrial Europe, notably about Prussia in the eighteenth century and about England in the seventeenth

(Rosenberg, 1958; Aylmer, 1961, 1973). To do this is to become aware that there was a long-term trend towards a bureaucratic system, but also that change was very slow. Seventeenth-century France, the France of Richelieu and Colbert, Le Tellier and Louvois, was on Weber's criteria one of the most bureaucratic states in Europe, but many patrimonial practices persisted. Richelieu, for example, treated official documents as if they were his private property, and left many of them to his niece in his will. He chose his subordinates on personal rather than impersonal grounds; that is, he did not look for the most able man to fill a given post, but tried to place one of his followers, his clients, his 'creatures' as they said in the seventeenth century (Ranum, 1963). Had he not operated in this way, he might not have survived politically. He needed subordinates he could trust and, apart from relatives, he could only trust his creatures, just as princes could only trust their favourites (see above, p. 51). Hence historians of the government of pre-industrial Europe must not only show when and why bureaucracy emerged, but also analyse how the patrimonial system worked. In this area the social anthropologists, who are much concerned with the mechanics of patronage and faction, may be of more help to historians than Weber, who stopped at the descriptive stage.

PATRONS, CLIENTS AND FACTIONS

Patronage may be defined as a political system based on personal relationships between unequals, between leaders (patrons) and their followers (clients). Each has something to give the other. Clients offer patrons their loyal support and also their deference, expressed in a variety of symbolic forms. Patrons, for their part, offer their clients protection from the demands of other patrons and also more positive favours, from hospitality to jobs. For a vivid description combined with a penetrating analysis of the workings of this system in a mid-twentieth-century society, we may turn to Fredrik Barth's account of the Swat Pathans. In this society the leaders, or *khans*, compete for land and follow-ers. They spend their wealth on gifts and hospitality in order to build up a following. The authority of each *khan* is personal, it is what he can 'wrest' from each of his follow-ers. 'Followers seek those leaders who offer them the great-est advantages and the most security.' The support of the clients gives the *khans* their following and thus gives them honour (*izat*), and the power to humiliate their rivals and to do favours for their clients in return for their loyalty. On the other hand, the need to keep their followers loyal forces the leaders to compete with one another. In Pathan society, where 'face' matters, a *khan* under pressure will increase his hospitality, even though his income may be declining and he has to sell land to feed the visitors. As one of them remarked to the visiting anthropologist, 'Only this constant show of force keeps the vultures at bay' (Barth, 1959, ch. 7).

The existence of patron-client relationships in political life is not news to historians of early modern Europe. It is thirty years since J. E. Neale described the Elizabethan political scene in terms of the rivalry between great men like Leicester and Norfolk, Essex and the Cecils, each of them the centre of a patronage network (Neale, 1948). It is commonplace to describe political struggles in early modern Europe in terms of 'faction', where faction means what it does for social anthropologists, a group of clients around a patron, a group united not by a common ideology but by a common relationship to a leader. Where Barth's analysis of the Swat Pathans may be of value to the histor-ian is in his emphasis on the order underlying the apparent disorder, and on the pressures on each of the actors, the leaders no less than the followers, to keep on playing his role.

If we turn to England in the fifteenth century, more especially to the East Anglia revealed in the Paston Letters, we find a society which in certain respects is not unlike that of the Pathans. In East Anglia as in Swat the competition for land sometimes took a violent form, as in the case of Lord Moleyns's seizure of John Paston's manor of Gresham. There is an unequal relationship between leaders ('lords' or 'masters') and followers ('friends' or 'well willers'). Followers court leaders with deference and even with gifts; as one correspondent remarks, 'men do not lure hawks with empty hands'. The small men need the 'good lordship' of the great. On the other hand, leaders need followers for the sake of their honour or 'worship' (which corresponds to *izat*), and so hand out liveries and keep open house. This was the system English historians have come to call 'bastard feudalism' (McFarlane, 1943 – 5). Turning to Lawrence Stone's account of the Elizabethan peerage, we find him emphasising their expenditure on hospitality but explaining it away as 'simply in order to justify the existence of echoing halls and sumptuous state apartments, and to keep at bay the melancholia and loneliness of a half empty mansion' (Stone, 1965, see esp. pp. 555 – 62). A reading of Fredrik Barth suggests a possible alternative explanation, as does a reading of Marcel Mauss's famous study of the gift in archaic societiès, a study which points out that in these societies there is no such thing as a 'free' gift. There is an obligation to give, an obligation to receive, and an obligation to make a return to the giver (Mauss, 1925). Could the Elizabethan patronage networks described by Neale have existed without the hospitality condemned by Stone? If some peers kept open house when they could ill afford it, they were perhaps acting from the same motives as the *khan* who tried by this means to keep the vultures at bay.

MENTALITY AND IDEOLOGY

The patron-client system depends, as we have seen, on the desire for honour and the fear of shame. The bureaucratic system also depends on a particular ethos. In each case it is impossible to understand how the system works if one does not understand the values of the participants. In other words, there can be no social history without the history of ideas, provided that that phrase is understood as the history of everyone's ideas rather than the ideas of the most original thinkers of a given epoch. If historians are interested in the attitudes and values of everyone in a particular society, they are likely to find two concepts useful in their research; mentality and ideology.

The mentalities approach is essentially the Durkheim approach to ideas, although Durkheim's own favourite term was 'collective representations', while contemporary sociologists and anthropologists use terms like 'belief systems', 'modes of thought', or 'cognitive maps'. The point of all these concepts is to emphasise the fact that people in different societies think in different ways; that is, they make different assumptions and use different categories to interpret experience. This is not to assume that there are no important differences of opinion within a given society. The study of 'collective mentalities', to use the French historians' term for this approach, simply concentrates on the attitudes which the members of that society have in common. Historians of mentalities are concerned with change, but only change over the long term, for societies do not change their modes of thought in a hurry (Le Goff, 1974).

The pioneering study in the history of mentalities was the work of Marc Bloch, who investigated the belief in the miraculous power attributed to the kings of France and England, the power to cure a skin disease (scrofula) by touching the sufferer. This belief persisted for centuries despite the fact that the expected cures failed to take place. Bloch's explanation for this persistence was that people expected a miracle, and so persuaded themselves that it must have happened (Bloch, 1923). The next important study of this type was also French. It was Lucien Febvre's book on the religion of Rabelais, which argued that atheism was impossible in the sixteenth century because the mentality or 'mental equipment' of the period did not permit it. He went on to inventory the most important items of that equipment, such as conceptions of causality, space and time, the ordinary and the marvellous (Febvre, 1942).

The history of mentalities has been relatively slow to attract British historians and it has come to them by a relatively roundabout route. The British anthropologist

Edward Evans-Pritchard was interested in the 'collective representations' of Durkheim and his followers, and adopted a similar approach in his study of the belief system of the Azande, a people of central Africa. Evans-Pritchard emphasised the self-confirming character of the Zande belief in their poison oracles in a way reminiscent of Bloch (whom he had also read) on the royal touch. 'In this web of belief, every strand depends upon every other strand, and a Zande cannot get out of its meshes because it is the only world he knows' (Evans-Pritchard, 1937). Through the social anthropology of Evans-Pritchard and his pupils (notably Mary Douglas), a concern with modes of thought or belief systems is now beginning to affect the approach of British historians to subjects such as witchcraft, magic and religion in England in the sixteenth and seventeenth centuries (Thomas, 1971; Bossy, 1975).

Like Durkheim, Bloch and Febvre studied rituals, like touching for the 'king's evil', as well as verbal expressions of communal values. The history of public rituals is now a growing field of historical research in Britain as in France. For example, a study of Coventry in the late Middle Ages emphasises the importance in civic life of the annual processions at Corpus Christi and Midsummer and of the Hock Tuesday play, and argues that these rituals both symbolised and helped to maintain the social structure of the city (Phythian-Adams, 1972). Two recent French books describe the new festivals which replaced traditional Catholic rituals after 1789, and the way in which these new forms expressed new attitudes and values (Ozouf, 1976; Vovelle, 1976).

This interest in collective attitudes and public rituals is one of the most important developments in the writing of history in recent years, and the seam is very far from being worked out. However, this 'mentalities' approach does have its dangers and difficulties, two in particular. One is that success in accounting for the persistence of traditional attitudes has its price, the difficulty of accounting for change. How do people struggle free from the 'web of belief'? If atheism is literally unthinkable in one period, how does it become possible in the next? The second difficulty is that this approach, true to its Durkheimian origin, assumes a consensus in society and shows little concern with conflict (cf. the analysis of the coronation, above, p. 44). Febvre cheerfully discussed the attitudes of 'the sixteenth-century Frenchman' as if variations between social groups did not matter. Bloch did not ask whether it was in the interest of any group in mediaeval France that people should believe that the king could work miracles. Public rituals express official values, but it is always worth asking whether there may be contrary values current unofficially in the same society.

Questions of this kind are, of course, central to the Marxist approach to beliefs in terms of ideology. 'Ideology' is a word with many definitions, but it is commonly used in two senses. The first is to suggest that a particular set of ideas or outlook is associated with a particular social class, with the implication that Febvre was wrong to discuss 'the' mentality of the sixteenth-century Frenchman and should have distinguished the attitudes of the nobility (say) from those of the bourgeoisie. This is what Karl Mannheim called the 'total' conception of ideology. The alternative, which he called the 'particular' conception of ideology, is the notion that ideas can be used to justify or 'legitimate' and so to maintain in being a particular social order. We return to the notion of 'symbolic violence' (above, p. 56; Mannheim, 1936; Bourdieu, 1972).

An example of historical analysis utilising the 'total' approach is Lucien Goldmann's interpretation of Jansenism as the ideology of the French *noblesse de robe* in the seventeenth century. Goldmann focuses on the rejection of the world by Jansenist writers such as Pascal and explains the appeal of this idea to French lawyers and officials by arguing that they were caught in an impossible dilemma, in conflict with the Crown yet dependent on the Crown, so that the rejection of the world seemed the only way out (Goldmann, 1955). As an example of the 'particular' approach to ideology we might take a recent analysis of the criminal law in eighteenth-century England, since a legal system is the institutionalisation of ideas about right and wrong. It has been argued that the gentry, who were also the magistrates, manipulated the penal code to their own advantage, but also that they were aware that their position depended on other people believing in the justice as well as the strength of their rule; that is, believing in the legitimacy of their authority (Hay, 1975).

An invaluable corrective to the idea of communal consensus, the concept of ideology also has its dangers. It encourages its users to blur certain distinctions which are well worth making. Is a particular outlook or world view necessarily associated with a particular social class, or does it simply happen to be the view held by the majority of its members at a particular period? If necessarily associated, how do the attitudes of that class ever change? Does a ruling class ever share a common set of values without dissent? Do its members manipulate other social groups consciously or unconsciously? Does the ruling class accept legal or religious restraints on its own behaviour or not? Do all the ideas current in a given society serve to justify the social order, or are some ideas (scientific, perhaps, or aesthetic) autonomous? The trouble with the concept of ideology is that it encourages, though it does not necessitate, a crude form of reductionism in which religion, law and other forms of culture are seen simply as a mechanism for keeping the ruling class in power.

It is to avoid this reductionism that some theorists have replaced the concept of ideology with that of cultural 'hegemony', a term used by the Italian Marxist Antonio Gramsci to refer to the acceptance by the subordinate classes of the culture of the ruling class, without either rulers or ruled necessarily being aware of the political consequences or functions of this acceptance. 'What is decisive', as Raymond Williams puts it in his exposition of the concept, 'is not only the conscious system of ideas and beliefs, but the whole lived social process as practically organised by specific and dominant meanings and values', organised in such a way that 'the pressures and limits of what can ultimately be seen as a specific economic, political and cultural system seem to most of us the pressures and limits of simple experience and common sense' (Williams, 1977, pp. 108 – 14).

The idea of cultural hegemony is at the point of convergence between historians operating with a 'mentalities' approach and historians thinking in terms of ideology. Among the historians currently trying to combine what is most valuable in the two approaches are two Frenchmen, Georges Duby and Michel Vovelle. Duby, a mediaevalist who owes a good deal to Marc Bloch and something to Louis Althusser, has made a study of the 'three estates' (those who pray, those who fight and those who work) as part of the ideology of mediaeval society rather than as an accurate description of its structure. He is particularly interested in the coexistence of different 'systems of representations' in the same society, in the problem of how new ones come into being, and in the way in which cultural models move down the social scale (Duby, 1968, 1978). Vovelle has done research on religious attitudes in eighteenth-century Provence, and on attitudes to death in particular. He presents his conclusions as a contribution to the history of mentalities, but he does not generalise about 'the eighteenth-century Provençal'. On the contrary, his meticulously statistical study of tens of thousands of wills has revealed important variations in attitudes to death, variations between different parts of Provence and also between different social groups. There were also significant changes in the course of the century. An ostentatious, 'baroque' devotion gave place to religious behaviour which was certainly less ostentatious and possibly less devout, less Christian. In this case, as in Duby's Middle Ages, cultural models can be seen moving down the social scale (Vovelle, 1973).

The problem of cultural diffusion leads naturally to the question of social change. The conceptual tool kit presented in this chapter has been discussed with reference to concrete historical problems but with relatively little reference to change over time. The problems of conceptualising change, structural change in particular, are the subject of the next chapter.

3

Social Change

The last chapter, concerned with structure, naturally emphasised what historians can learn from sociology. Here the stress will fall on what sociologists can learn from history. Historians might be said to have two contributions to make to the theory of social change, one negative and one positive.

The negative contribution is for the historian to specify how a particular model of social change, all-embracing in principle, fails in practice to fit 'his' particular society, and in what respects it needs to be modified. Here we see a process of working inwards from general to particular, with the historian chipping away at generalisations like a sculptor attacking a block of marble. The positive contribution involves the historian in modelling rather than sculpting, building up rather than breaking down, working outwards from general to particular, giving an account of the process of change in one society which might help in the construction of a revised general model.

But what exactly is social change? The term is an ambiguous one. In its narrower sense it may be defined as 'a change in social structure, for example the size of a society, the composition or balance of its parts, or the type of its organisation' (Ginsberg, 1958). In its wider sense the term embraces the processes of economic, political and cultural change – in other words, any alteration in structure. This chapter will centre on the narrow definition, but it will stray on occasion into the periphery.

Like philosophies of history, from which they cannot be completely distinguished, models of social change fall into a number of main types. Either they are cyclical, like

Sorokin's model of social and cultural 'fluctuations', or Toynbee's, or Spengler's, or the models current at the Renaissance, and in ancient Greece and Rome; or they are linear, like the Judaeo-Christian and Marxist philosophies of history. Either they stress internal factors of change, and use organic metaphors like 'growth', 'evolution', 'sickness', or 'decay', or they place the emphasis on external factors and use terms like 'diffusion', 'borrowing' and 'imitation'. At the beginning of this century, diffusionist models were popular. They were favoured not only by archaeologists and anthropologists but also by such sociologists as Gabriel Tarde, whose book *The Laws of Imitation* (1890) involved him in controversy with Durkheim, and Thorstein Veblen, whose study of *Imperial Germany and the Industrial Revolution* (1915) centred on the concept of 'borrowing'. Since diffusionism is often condemned nowadays as a superficial and mechanical theory, it may be worth stressing the fact that in the hands of Tarde and Veblen it was neither. Both men were interested in differences in receptivity to innovation. Veblen, for example, discussed the special 'propensity to borrow' of the Germans, the Scandinavians and the Japanese.

However, in a short chapter it is probably better to confine historical chipping to the two principal models of social change currently in use, the conflict model and the modernisation model, Marx and Spencer.

SPENCER'S MODEL

'Spencer' is a convenient piece of shorthand for the 'modernisation' model, which emphasises its concern with social 'evolution'. Social evolution might be defined as social change which is gradual and cumulative ('evolution' as opposed to 'revolution'); essentially determined from within ('endogenous' as opposed to 'exogenous'); and involves what is often called 'structural differentiation', a shift from the simple, unspecialised and informal to the complex, specialised and formal, or in Spencer's own words from 'incoherent homogeneity' to 'coherent hetero-geneity'. Roughly speaking, this is the model of social change employed by Durkheim and Weber.

Durkheim, who disagreed with Spencer on many points, followed him in describing social change in essentially evolutionary terms. He saw it as the gradual replacement of simple 'mechanical solidarity' (the solidarity of the similar), by complex 'organic solidarity' (the solidarity of the complementary), thanks to the increasing division of labour in society (Durkheim, 1893; cf. Lukes, 1973, ch. 7). Weber, on the other hand, tended to avoid the word 'evolu-tion', but all the same he interpreted world history in terms of the gradual yet irreversible trend towards more rational, complex and impersonal forms of social organisation such as capitalism and bureaucracy. It is thus not too difficult to make a synthesis of Weber and Durkheim on social change, and this is precisely what has been done by contemporary theorists of modernisation such as Talcott Parsons.

It would be unfair to present their theory in simplified form and then proceed to criticise it for oversimplification. Parsons has on occasion distinguished between five types of society, in an evolutionary sequence from 'primitive' through 'advanced primitive', 'archaic' and 'advanced intermediate', to 'modern' (Parsons, 1966). Yet it would not be unfair to say that theorists of modernisation have tended to present 'traditional society' and 'modern society' as two antithetical types on the following lines. The social hierarchy of 'traditional society' is based on birth ('ascrip-tion'), and social mobility is low. In 'modern society', by contrast, the hierarchy is based on achievement and mobility is high (compare the distinction between 'estates' and 'classes', above, p. 63f). In traditional society, everyone lives in a face-to-face community (*Gemeinschaft*). After modernisation, everyone lives in an impersonal society (*Gesellschaft*) and social life is organised by forming a variety of voluntary associations for specific ends. In tradi-tional society, people are unaware of change or hostile to it, and actions are legitimated in terms of custom and prece-dent. In modern society, people are well aware of change and actions are legitimated in terms of progress. To these basic distinctions all sorts of contrasts have been added. Some sociologists have suggested that the culture of traditional society is oral, religious and magical, while the culture of modern society is literate, secular and scientific, and that the extended family is dominant in the first type of society, while the nuclear family is dominant in the second.

The process by which societies of the first type have given way to societies of the second is generally seen as a process of development from within in which the external environment enters only to provide a stimulus to 'adaptation'. Social change is summarised in terms of urbanisation, secularisation and structural differentiation. However, it is recognised that the different sectors of society do not change at the same rate. Since society is composed of mutually dependent parts, a change in one sector requires changes in others, and until these changes take place there is a temporary maladjustment or 'cultural lag' (Ogburn, 1923, pp. 200 – 1).

The links between this model of social change and current models of economic growth and political development will be obvious enough. Theorists of economic growth have emphasised the 'take-off' from a static pre-industrial society to a dynamic industrial one in which growth is the normal condition and 'Compound interest becomes built, as it were, into its habits and institutional structure' (Rostow, 1960). Theorists of political development note the rise of political 'participation' (or to use a more old-fashioned term, 'democracy'), as well as the rise of bureaucracy studied by Weber.

Historians are not the only people to see defects in this model, but historians of complex traditional societies such as Augustan Rome, Ming China and Bourbon France are likely to be particularly ill at ease with 'Spencer'. The model was elaborated in the 1950s with special reference to change in the 'underdeveloped' countries (as they were called at the time), and with some reference to industrialisation in the nineteenth century, but with little thought for history before 1800. 'Traditional society' was something of a residual category, defined as the opposite of the sociologist's own society. It is scarcely surprising that historians of pre-industrial Europe should have found that the model does not fit the societies they study. They have expressed three kinds of misgiving in particular; doubts about the direction, the mechanics and the explanation of social change according to the model.

In the first place, social change is not always a movement from simplicity to complexity. History is not a 'one-way street' (Stone, 1977, p. 666). Since the Industrial Revolution, social trends have usually been trends towards complexity, but it would surely be a mistake to found a universal theory on a mere two centuries of world history. Specialists in earlier periods have no difficulty in pointing to changes in the opposite direction. Historians of the later Roman Empire and the 'barbarian invasions' generally discuss social change in terms of the decline of the towns, the decentralisation or breakdown of government, and the replacement of secular attitudes by other-worldly ones, thus turning modernisation on its head. Historians of Spain and Italy in the sixteenth and seventeenth centuries have suggested that these societies were becoming less mobile, moving from achievement to ascription instead of the other way round. Historians of Eastern Europe in the same period note a decline rather than a rise of towns, trade and the bourgeoisie. In short, the fact that 'urbanisation', 'secularisation' and, above all, 'structural differentiation' are process-words without opposites tells us more about the assumptions of sociologists than about the nature of social change.

The term 'modernisation' gives the impression of a linear process, but intellectual historians are well aware that the word 'modern' (which was already in use in the period we call the 'Middle Ages') has had very different meanings at different times. The way in which the concept was used by Ranke and Burckhardt, who believed that modernisation ('modern history') began in the fifteenth century, seems curiously old-fashioned today. Ranke stressed state-building and Burckhardt stressed individualism; neither of them had anything to say about industrialisation. Having inherited this tradition, twentieth-century historians have been forced to coin the self-contradictory term 'early modern' to refer to the period between the end of the Middle Ages and the beginning of the Industrial Revolution. The trouble with modernity is that it keeps changing.

A more precise criticism of some versions of the Spencer model centres on its interpretation of the history of the family, especially in Europe, as a story of gradual contraction from the 'clan' (in the sense of a large group of kin) in the early Middle Ages, through the joint or stem family in early modern times to the conjugal or nuclear family characteristic of industrial society. This theory of 'progressive nuclearisation' has been challenged by historians, notably by Peter Laslett, who has pointed out that household size in England scarcely varied from a mean of 4.75 between the sixteenth and the nineteenth centuries, and, more generally, that households of this size have long been characteristic of most of Europe and also of Japan (Laslett, 1972).

Household size is not the only way of measuring family units (see above, p. 54), and a revised version of the nuclearisation theory has been put forward for England by Lawrence Stone, who argues that the 'open lineage family' dominant in the late fifteenth and early sixteenth centuries was replaced first by the 'restricted patriarchal nuclear family', and then, in the eighteenth century, by the 'closed domesticated nuclear family' (Stone, 1977). But this view is questioned by Alan Macfarlane, who argues that not only the nuclear family, but also wage labour and individual ownership, were to be found in England as early as the thirteenth century; in other words, that mediaeval England was 'a capitalist-market economy without factories' (Macfarlane, 1978). This conclusion suggests that we should not be thinking in terms of the consequences of industrialisation for society so much as of the fit between social structure and industrialisation. Traditional social structures seem to have been more diverse and also more resilient to change than the modernisation model allows.

In the second place, historians confronted with this model have expressed doubts about the mechanics of social change. Do changes in the same general direction necessarily follow the same path? The Spencer model makes little reference to the mechanics of change, and this lack of explicit discussion encourages the assumption of unilinearity. It makes the process of modernisation appear to be a smooth, uniform and virtually automatic sequence of stages, as if all different societies had to do was to step on to the escalator. Rostow's study of the five stages of economic growth, from 'the traditional society', through the 'take-off' to 'the age of high mass-consumption', is an unusually explicit example of the escalator model. It may be contrasted with the approach of the economic historian Alexander Gershenkron. In his famous essay on 'economic backwardness in historical perspective', Gershenkron argued that late industrialisers, like Russia, did not fit the model of early industrialisers, like Britain. In the later cases the role of the state was greater and the role of the profit motive was less. Latecomers could not follow the earlier model precisely because they were latecomers, in a hurry to catch up with the early industrialisers (Gershenkron, 1951; Rostow, 1960).

Again, in his communications model of modernisation, a variant of Spencer, Daniel Lerner has asserted (1958, p. 46) that

Everywhere ... increasing urbanisation has tended to raise literacy; rising literacy has tended to increase media exposure; increasing media exposure has 'gone with' wider economic participation (per capita income) and political participation (voting) ... the same basic model reappears in virtually all modernising societies.

It is a pity that these hypotheses, which Lerner illustrates from the Middle East in the twentieth century, have not been picked up and tested by historians. On the face of it there is more than one European case which does not fit the model. Seventeenth-century Naples, with a population of half a million, was a case of urbanisation without much literacy or 'participation'. Eighteenth-century Sweden, on the other hand, had 90 per cent literacy without urbanisation. The mechanics of modernisation must be more complex than Lerner suggests.

Similar problems arise, as E. A. Wrigley has pointed out, if industrialisation is treated as the key variable in the modernisation process. In the middle of the eighteenth century, part of the Dutch Republic was modern (in the 'structural differentiation' sense) without being industrial (in the sense of having towns and factories). The Veluwe was a rural area with a working population involved in the production of textiles and paper as well as in agriculture. Conversely, in the north of England in the early nineteenth century, there was industrialisation without modernisation, in the sense that factories and towns coexisted with illiteracy and a strong sense of community (Wrigley, 1972 – 3). Social change seems to be multilinear rather than unilinear. There is more than one path to modernity. Nor is this path necessarily smooth. France from 1789 onwards and Russia from 1917 on are obvious examples of cases where it is difficult to describe the process of social change without using the term 'crisis' to refer to the collapse of traditional social as well as political structures under the impact of revolutionary events.

In the third place, historians have doubts about the explanation of social change built into the Spencer model. The model suggests that change is basically internal to a given social system. It represents the development of potential, the growth of a branching tree. However, it is not difficult for historians to cite examples of social change in the past which do not fit this internalist model. Conquests, for example. The Norman Conquest has been described as 'the classic example in European history of the disruption of a social order by the sudden introduction of an alien military technology' (White, 1962, p. 38). Outside Europe, the Spanish conquest of Mexico and Peru and the British conquest of India are equally classic examples of social change induced from without. Epidemics illustrate a different kind of penetration from outside. In 1348, for example, the Black Death invaded Europe from Asia and killed about a third of the population. The consequent manpower shortages led to important long-term changes in the European social structure. In all these cases, the violent impact of forces from outside the society in question makes it inappropriate to discuss them in terms of mere stimuli to adaptation, which is the only function allotted to external factors in the Spencer model.

It should be added, to be fair, that some theorists of modernisation are aware of all these problems and that they have reconstructed or 'modernised' the model in order to deal with objections. S. N. Eisenstadt finds a place in his version of the model both for 'external pressures' and for 'regression to decentralisation' (Eisenstadt, 1963, 1973). It is even more important to add that long before the vogue of modernisation theory in the 1950s, Norbert Elias had published a study of what he called the 'sociogenesis of Western civilisation', putting forward a theory of social change which owes something to the Spencer tradition but is not vulnerable to the three objections which have just been stated. Elias distinguished 'two main directions in the structural changes of society...those tending toward increased differentiation and integration, and those tending toward decreased differentiation and integration'. He had a good deal to say about the mechanics of change, noting, for example, that social integration was an unintended consequence of the competition for power between small states in the Middle Ages. If he analysed social development in essentially internal terms, he looked at it on a European scale and was aware of the impact of one region on others (Elias, 1939).

The Spencer model is not necessarily unhistorical, and it would be a real loss if the historical profession were to reject all versions of it without noticing the insights they embody and the connections they suggest. In recent years a few historians have in fact found the model to be of some use. A study of the Roman Empire, for example, discusses the parallel rise of the professional soldier, the professional lawyer and the professional teacher as three aspects of the process of structural differentiation (Hopkins, 1978, pp. 74 – 96). A history of Irish society since the Great Famine is organised round the concept of modernisation, defined in terms of increasing equality of opportunity, in the hope that this term will 'prove immune to the parochial preoccupations implicit in equally elusive and more emotive concepts like gaelicisation and anglicisation.' Sociology's comparative perspective here allows the general to be seen in the particular (Lee, 1973). German historians have been turning to the modernisation model as a way of conceptualising social changes in German states in the late eighteenth and early nineteenth centuries. The growth of voluntary associations in this period, associations founded for a variety of highly specific aims, has been interpreted as part of the general process of change from a traditional 'estate society' to a modern, individualist, democratic 'class society' (Nipperdey, 1972). In the last case we see something of a conceptual circular tour, since it was on the basis of German social history that Weber formulated the distinction between 'estates' and 'classes' which was later incorporated into modernisation theory. However, it might be fruitful to study not only German clubs but also French fraternities and drinking societies, and English trade unions and friendly societies, as part of a process of structural differentiation.

MARX'S MODEL

'Marx', like 'Spencer', is a convenient piece of shorthand which will be used here to refer to a model of social change to which Engels, Lenin, Lukács and Gramsci (among others) all made contributions. In a sentence, it may be described as a model of a sequence of societies ('social formations') derived from modes of production, and containing internal contraditions which lead to class conflict, crisis, social revolution and discontinuous change. In some ways this model is not unlike its main rival. Like Spencer, Marx includes the idea of a sequence of forms of society –

tribal, slave, feudal, capitalist, communist. Feudalism and capitalism, the social formations which have been discussed most, are virtually defined as opposites of one another, like traditional and modern society. Like Spencer, Marx explains social change in fundamentally endogenous terms, by the internal dynamic of the mode of production. However, in some of its versions at least, the Marx model does stand up to the three main historical criticisms of Spencer.

In the first place, Marx makes some allowance for the possibility of change in the 'wrong' direction, change which is described as 'refeudalisation', or, more recently, as 'the development of underdevelopment'. Marxists have often discussed the fact that the rise of the bourgeoisie and the towns in Western Europe in the sixteenth century not only coincided with, but actually led to, the decline of the bourgeoisie and the towns in Eastern Europe. On one side of the Elbe, the rise of capitalism; on the other, what Engels called the 'second serfdom'. The two sequences were in fact complementary. The development of one area, exporting manufactured goods, depended on the 'underdevelopment' of the other, which now concentrated on exporting raw materials. It was a case of the division of labour (Wallerstein, 1974; cf. Frank, 1967).

In the second place, Marx is much more concerned than Spencer with the mechanics of social change, especially in the case of the transition from feudalism to capitalism. Change is viewed in dialectical terms; that is, with the emphasis on conflict and on consequences which are not only unintended but the very opposite of what was planned. Relations of production which once unleashed productive forces 'turn into their fetters'. The bourgeoisie dig their own graves by calling the proletariat into existence. Structures do not change automatically, as they seem to do in the Spencer model; on the contrary, political events, notably revolutions, are part of the process of change. On the question of unilinear versus multilinear development, there is disagreement. Marx himself considered the tribal-slave-feudal-capitalist-socialist schema relevant to European history alone. He did not expect Russia, or even India, to follow the Western path, although he did not say what paths he did expect them to take. Some recent writers within the Marx tradition are firmly multilinear. Barrington Moore distinguishes three main historical routes to the modern world: bourgeois revolution, as in England, France or the USA (the 'classic' route); conservative revolution, as in the cases of Prussia and Japan; and peasant revolution, as in Russia and China. Again, Perry Anderson emphasises the variety of possible paths to modernity by choosing the metaphor 'trajectory' in preference to that of 'evolution', and by calling his two volumes 'passages' from antiquity to feudalism and 'lineages' of the absolutist state (Moore, 1966; Anderson, 1974a, 1974b).

Thirdly and finally, there is a place in Marx for 'exogenous' explanations of social change. In the case of the West, this place is generally agreed to be a subordinate one. In the famous controversy among Marxists in the 1950s over the transition from feudalism to capitalism, Paul Sweezy's explanation of the decline of feudalism by external factors such as the reopening of the Mediterranean and the consequent growth of trade and towns met with a chorus of rejection (Hilton, 1976). On the other hand, Marx himself regarded Asian society as devoid of internal mechanisms of change. The function or, as he put it, the 'mission' of the British in India was to destroy the traditional social framework and so to make change possible (Avineri, 1968). Where Spencer presents modernisation as a series of parallel developments in different areas, Marx offers a more global account which stresses connections between changes in one society and changes in others (Frank, 1967; Wallerstein, 1974).

The Marx model seems to stand up to the criticisms of historians rather better than the Spencer model. This is not altogether surprising. The model has been well known to historians for a long time, and many of them have modified it. It is not difficult to think of historical classics built on a Marxist framework, like E. P. Thompson's *Making of the English Working Class* (1963), or Maurice Agulhon's *The*

Republic in the Village (1970), a study of eastern Provence in the first half of the nineteenth century, or Emilio Sereni's *Capitalism in the Countryside* (1947), a study of Italy in the generation after unification.

It may not be coincidence that all three books, and most of the others which might have been cited, deal with Marx's own century, and with the social transformation he knew and analysed best, the rise of capitalism, accompanied by the polarisation of society, increasing class-consciousness and political action from below. The Marx model is considerably less satisfactory as an interpretation of pre-industrial old regimes. It does not, for example, specify sufficiently the nature of social conflict before the development of class-consciousness. In practice, Marxist historians of old regimes tend to offer a weak version of their model when what is needed is a modified version. For example, social conflict in seventeenth-century France has been presented as a foreshadowing of the class conflicts which led to the revolution of 1848, as if they were different in degree rather than in kind (see above, p. 64). It is only recently that Marxist historians have taken serious account of social solidarities other than class-consciousness (Hobsbawm, 1971a; E. P. Thompson, 1978). Another serious deficiency in the Marx model of social change in pre-industrial societies is its lack of emphasis (till a few years ago) on demographic factors, which may well have been the most important motors of change in that period (see below, p. 98f.).

The Marx model, with its stress on conflict as the means by which social change comes about, and the Spencer model, with its emphasis on evolution and adaptation, obviously complement one another. Is a synthesis possible? It has not been achieved, but there are signs of convergence. Barrington Moore's comparative study of the role of landlords and peasants in 'the making of the modern world' is a fundamentally Marxist account, but contaminated by modernisation theory and all the more penetrating for its lack of purity. Moore's former pupil Charles Tilly is an example of convergence from the other side. He is a 'moderniser' more aware than most of the criticisms which Marxists make of this approach, and conscious in particular of the need to relate changes within a given society to changes in its relationship with the rest of the world (Moore, 1966; Tilly, 1964, 1975).

However, a synthesis of Marx with Spencer, even if this were possible without self-contradiction, would not deal with all the objections which have come up so far. The two models share serious limitations of perspective. They are both primarily concerned to account for industrialisation and its consequences, and are at their best when doing just that. They are much less satisfactory in their account of changes before the middle of the eighteenth century. 'Traditional society' in Spencer, and 'feudal society' in Marx, are residual categories, looking-glass worlds in which the principal characteristics of 'modern' or 'capitalist' society are to be found in reverse. This is not difficult to understand – people so often interpret the 'other' as the opposite of themselves – but it does not make for a realistic analysis of the pre-industrial world.

Of course, no model of social change is ever going to satisfy historians completely, because of their professional interest in variety. It is in this sense that, as Ronald Dore puts it, 'You can't make sociological omelettes without breaking a few historical eggs'. Hexter's attack on Marxism as a 'prefabricated theory of social change' is really an attack on all theories, on all models (Hexter, 1955). Other historians accept the need for models but are unhappy with all the models available. One British social historian recently denounced the quest for a 'short-cut theoretical salvation in sociology' on the grounds that 'theoretical work in history is too important to be subcontracted to others' (Stedman Jones, 1976). Without going as far as this, either in rejecting what sociologists have done or in expecting historians to come up with a theory, I should now like to discuss the possibility of working outwards from a few monographs on the history of complex traditional societies. A model of social change which took more account of such societies would not only be useful to many historians, but also a better, because more generally applicable, model.

FOUR MONOGRAPHS IN SEARCH OF A THEORY

The four books to be discussed all treat problems of social change in particular societies in an explicit and self-conscious manner. All four deal with the history of Europe, or with Europeans outside Europe, in the early modern period; but classical, mediaeval or oriental examples could equally well have been chosen.

The oldest and the most famous of these four monographs is Fernand Braudel's study *The Mediterranean and the Mediterranean World in the Age of Philip II*. The point which Braudel was most concerned to make in this huge book was not about Philip II or even about the Mediterranean, so much as about the nature of time. He suggests that changes take place at different speeds, and that it is useful to distinguish three of these speeds in particular. He devotes a section of his book to each. There is the fast-moving time of events, the subject of traditional narrative history (*histoire événementielle*); the time of 'economic systems, states, societies and civilisations', with its 'slow but perceptible rhythms' (*histoire conjoncturelle*); and finally, the history of man in relation to his environment, 'a history whose passage is almost imperceptible . . . a history of constant repetition, ever-recurring cycles' (*histoire structurale*).

It is the first part of the book, devoted to the history of the environment ('geohistory', as Braudel sometimes calls it), which is the most revolutionary, but it is the second part which is most relevant here, dealing as it does with 'economic systems, states, societies and civilisations'. 'If the expression had not been diverted from its full meaning', writes Braudel, 'one could call it social history.' Social history in the wider of the two senses of social change discussed above (p. 80). In this part of his book, Braudel deals with the population explosion and the price revolution of the sixteenth century. He discusses political structures, suggesting that in this period, unlike the one which preceded and the one which followed it, history favoured large political units like the Ottoman and Habsburg empires. He has something to say about the diffusion of art and ideas and also about the resistance to diffusion, such as the resistance to Protestantism in the Mediterranean world. One section of the book deals with social change in the narrower sense of the term, with the history of the nobility, the bourgeoisie and the poor. Braudel's basic thesis is that the social distance between the rich and the poor was increasing in this period. In the later sixteenth century, in the Ottoman and Habsburg empires alike, 'society was tending to polarise itself into, on the one hand, a rich and vigorous nobility reconstituted into powerful dynasties owning vast properties, and on the other, the great and growing mass of the poor and dis-inherited'.

This last passage may sound not unlike Marx, for whom Braudel has considerable respect, but there is an important difference between their views of the sixteenth century. Braudel is not thinking in terms of the rise of the bour-geoisie. On the contrary, he is concerned with what he calls the 'defection of the bourgeoisie', or their 'bankruptcy' (*faillite de la bourgeoisie*). In this period the merchants of the Mediterranean world often turned their backs on trade, acquired land, behaved like noblemen and sometimes bought titles of nobility. In terms of modernisation theory, the period was less 'modern' than the one before it. In fact Braudel tends to think not in terms of progress but in terms of cycles, the alternation of phases of expansion and phases of contraction, 'A phases' and 'B phases', to use the language of François Simiand, an economist-historian of the early twentieth century who has had considerable influence in France. If *The Mediterranean* illustrates any sociological theory of change, it is surely that of Pareto, whose 'circulation of elites' involved the alternation of 'speculators' and 'rentiers', rather than that of Marx.

For a historian, one of the most obvious and at the same time one of the most fundamental criticisms of sociological models of change is that they are too shallow, in the sense of placing too much emphasis on the relatively short term, a generation, a mere thirty years or so. Despite its official concern with the reign of Philip II (1556 – 98), Braudel's is the most important single book to place on the other side of the scale. With it goes a short article in which Braudel makes more explicit his views on the importance of the long term (*la longue durée*), and tries to open a dialogue with the social sciences (Braudel, 1958).

William H. McNeill has also concerned himself with the history of the Ottoman Empire, but from a somewhat different point of view, concentrating on what he calls 'Europe's steppe frontier'. McNeill much admires Braudel, but his book owes at least as much to an American predecessor, Frederick Jackson Turner (see above, p. 24). It may be no accident that the book was written by a native of the Middle West.

McNeill's main theme is the changing relation between the centre and the periphery of the Ottoman Empire. It is on this framework that he constructs his model of social change. His thesis is that 'the centre could sustain organised military power on a large scale for an extended time only by preying upon peripheral communities while keeping a secure home base'. To do this meant that the empire was geared to continuous conquest. The booty thus collected saved the regime from having to oppress the peasantry of the central provinces. In addition – though McNeill does not emphasise this point as much as he might – the so-called 'tribute of children' collected from the subject Christian population allowed a centralised meritocratic system to function (see above, p. 69).

However, at some point the frontier had to close and conquest had to stop, if only for logistic reasons. 'The only effective limit upon the expansion of Turkish power', suggests McNeill, was the distance the sultan's army could travel to and from winter quarters for the campaigning season. However, in the late sixteenth century, the balance of power between the Ottoman and Habsburg empires produced conditions of stalemate. The frontier zone between the empires was ravaged by both sides, with the result that 'the very operations of the Turkish field armies tended ... to create conditions at the extreme range of their effective radius of action that prevented them from going further'. When expansion stopped, the political system began to disintegrate and the social structure had to change. The soldiers settled down on the land and 'the drive toward hereditary succession among the military elite of the empire gathered strength'. One might add that the supply of Christian children available for recruitment into the elite probably dwindled. At all events, sons began to succeed their fathers in the civilian elite as in the military one. Local notables emerged, and the political system became less centralised. Taxes replaced plunder as the chief source of revenue, so that the burdens on the peasantry increased. At this point McNeill seems to be describing some of the phenomena touched on by Braudel in his account of the polarisation of Mediterranean society, but he offers a different explanation, less economic and more political.

McNeill's might be described as a self-destructive model of social change. In a sense, such a model is implicit in all cyclical views of history, from Polybius to Toynbee. However, it is made explicit in this book, which gives a particularly clear account of the mechanics of change. Each phase of development follows from the one before. It is likely that this centre-periphery model will help in the analysis of the life-cycles of other empires; that of the Fort Jameson Ngoni, for instance. In the nineteenth century the Ngoni, we are told, 'depended largely on the efficiency of their army for the continual inflow of captives on which the strength and continued existence of the state depended ... As the Ngoni army increased in size, so it became easier for them to capture more people, so that what we may describe as an inflationary spiral in population was set up. The Ngoni state was like a snowball which grows larger and larger as it is pushed from place to place.' However, this empire too collapsed (Barnes, 1954).

The most brilliant of Braudel's pupils, Emmanuel Le Roy Ladurie, has studied social change over the long term in a Mediterranean region in his book *The Peasants of Languedoc*. Like Braudel, Le Roy Ladurie is fascinated by geography (he has written a history of climate), and by what he calls 'history without movement' (*l'histoire immobile*). However, his book might be more accurately described as 'ecohistory' than as 'geohistory', because its focus is on the history of social groups in relation to their environment. Le Roy Ladurie places more emphasis than Braudel on movements of population. In his model, which owes something to Malthus and Ricardo and something to contemporary social anthropology, it is above all demographic change, mediated by economic factors (and also by cultural factors, like mentalities), which leads to changes in the social structure.

Le Roy Ladurie's study of Languedoc is 'immobile' only in the limited sense that the province more or less returned to its point of departure at the end of what the author calls 'a great agrarian cycle, lasting from the end of the fifteenth century to the beginning of the eighteenth'. The basic pattern in this period is one of growth followed by decline. In phase A, the phase of expansion, there was a population explosion, followed by land clearance, the subdivision of farms, a price rise and a victory of profit, which meant a victory of the class living from profit, the entrepreneurs, at the expense of both rent and wages. In the seventeenth century, however, agricultural productivity hit a ceiling and all the main trends went into reverse in a classic example of a B phase. As the population began to press on the means of subsistence it stopped growing, and late in the seventeenth century actually declined, owing to famine, plague, emigration and, later, marriage. Profit was defeated by rent, the speculator (to use the language of Pareto) by the rentier. Holdings which had been fragmented were united once more. Looking at the period as a whole, it is clear that Languedoc functioned as a 'homeostatic eco-system'.

In this fundamentally ecological-demographic model there is also a place for culture. As Le Roy Ladurie puts it, 'The forces that first deflected the expansion, then checked it and ultimately broke it were not only economic in a narrow sense but also cultural' in a wide sense which includes 'the customs, the way of life, the mentality of a people'. Inheritance customs, for example. There was no primogeniture in Languedoc, so population growth necessarily involved the division of holdings. On the mentalities side, the author discusses the spread of literacy and Protestantism in Languedoc, with some reference to the Weber thesis about the interdependence of Protestantism and capitalism.

There is also a place in this model for the history of events, which are more closely integrated into Le Roy Ladurie's account of social change than they are into Braudel's. He focuses on social conflict and social protest in order to show how contemporaries perceived social change and how they reacted to it. In phase A, the phase of expansion, the reader hears about the carnival at Romans in Dauphiné in 1580, during which craftsmen and peasants declared that 'the rich of their town had grown rich at the expense of the poor people'. In phase B, the phase of contraction, Le Roy Ladurie discusses the revolt of the Vivarais in 1670, under the traditional slogan 'Long live the king, down with the tax-officials', as 'a more instinctive than rational reaction to the rural crisis'.

We are not left with the impression that these protests made any appreciable difference to the course of social change. However, in a discussion of a book on the politics of the Sarthe (a region in north-west France which votes for the right while its neighbours vote for the left), Le Roy Ladurie makes the point that events, in this case the local counter-revolution of 1793, can break traditional structures and create new ones which may then persist for centuries. The event may be a 'matrix' (Bois, 1960; Le Roy Ladurie, 1972).

If there is a general lesson to be drawn from the Languedoc book, it is that in pre-industrial societies the most important factor in social change is the growth or decline in population. This is a conclusion towards which a group of French historians, including Marxists like Pierre

Vilar and Guy Bois, have been moving (Vilar, 1962; Bois, 1976). The value for sociologists of Le Roy Ladurie's book on Languedoc, like Postan's study of mediaeval England, is in its presentation of a model of social change in which population plays a vital part (Postan, 1972).

The fourth and last case study to be discussed here is also French — Nathan Wachtel's *Vision of the Vanquished*. This analysis of the Spanish conquest of Peru is concerned with the 'crisis provoked by the conquest', and with the process of social change in Peru between 1530 and 1580. The key terms in Wachtel's model are 'destructuration' and 'acculturation'.

By 'destructuration' is meant the snapping of the links which made the different parts of the traditional social system into a whole. Traditional institutions and customs survived piecemeal after 1530, but the old structure disintegrated. Tribute survived, for example, but without the old system of redistribution by the state of which it had formed a part. Local chiefs survived, but their relation to the central government was no longer what it had been in the days of the Incas. Traditional religion survived, but became an unofficial, indeed a clandestine cult, regarded as 'idolatry' by the Spanish missionaries who did all they could to uproot it.

How did the Indians react to this destructuration process? Wachtel discusses their responses in terms of 'acculturation', which he defines (in an article which makes his model more explicit) as culture contact in a situation where one society is dominant and the other subordinate (Wachtel, 1974). Some of the Indians accepted the values of their conquerors, though apparent acceptance sometimes masks the persistence, conscious or unconscious, of traditional habits of thought. The chronicler Guaman Poma de Ayala, for example, inserted a good deal of Western information into his account of Peru, but the fundamental categories of his thought, such as his conceptions of space and time, remained indigenous. What is important here is not just objective culture contact but a subjective element, collectively subjective, that is, the subordinate culture's image of the conquerors' culture, the 'vision of the vanquished', as Wachtel calls it. The variety of reactions to the Spanish and their culture also needs to be stressed. Some Indians assimilated Spanish culture, while others resisted acculturation by revolt, as in the case of those who took part in the millenarian movement of Taqui Ongo in defence of the traditional gods. Others changed in order to stay the same, like the Araucans, who adopted the horse the better to resist the Spaniards who had introduced it.

It may seem odd to be proposing Wachtel's acculturation model for use by sociologists and anthropologists, given that the term 'acculturation' was originally coined by anthropologists (in the USA, in the late nineteenth century), and is no longer taken seriously by most of them (for an exception, see Foster, 1960, another exploration of the consequences of Spanish conquest). However, Wachtel is more than just an interesting case of disciplinary lag. As often happens in cases of disciplinary as well as culture contact, historians have transformed what they borrowed. Wachtel is no simple diffusionist. His concern for the social and political context of culture contact (drawing on Gramsci's theory of cultural hegemony), his distinction between cultural form (categories, schemata) and content (information), and his interest in the ways in which members of the two cultures perceive one another all give the old acculturation model a new, sharp cutting edge.

Wachtel's work converges with that of other anthropologists and historians. Walter Neale and Bernard Cohn have emphasised the part played in the process of social change in nineteenth-century India by the failure of the British to understand the nature of traditional Indian society. The *zamindars* for example, in a sense tax-collectors, were perceived and treated as landowners because the officials of the East India Company thought in terms of the British system of landlords and tenants. Misunderstanding of the social structure led to change in the social structure, as it had to, given the subjective element in social structure and the dominant position of the British (Neale, 1957; Cohn, 1960).

An interesting recent development is the adaptation of the acculturation model by French historians to the analysis of their own society. Robert Muchembled has discussed the 'acculturation of the rural world' in north-east France at the end of the sixteenth century, noting that the persecution of witches coincided with the Counter-Reformation attack on 'idolatry' and with the spread of literacy in the countryside. The centre was trying to convert the periphery, the rulers were attempting to change the values of the ruled. In that sense it is no far cry from Peru to the Cambrésis (Muchembled, 1978). In a similar manner *The Peasants of Languedoc* had described the revolt of the Protestants of the Cévennes at the beginning of the eighteenth century as a protest against 'deculturation' (Le Roy Ladurie, 1966). In their concern with destructuration and restructuration, Le Roy Ladurie and Wachtel seem to show the influence of the Italian sociologist Vittorio Lanternari (Lanternari, 1960, 1966).

These last examples may help to show that when historians reject the Marx and Spencer models of social change as too 'internalist', some of them at least have a positive alternative in mind.

This chapter began by working inwards from the difficulties in current models of social change, and continued by working outwards from case studies. Readers may still feel that the two tunnels have not met. They would be right. I am not offering a new model of social change, but simply a few points which might be taken into account in a future model. I should like to emphasise and elaborate three of these points by way of conclusion. They all concern the diversity of changes in society, a diversity which quickly becomes apparent once a longer period than the last century is taken into account.

The first point concerns the different directions of change. If movement in the direction of complexity, specialisation and centralisation is defined as 'forward', then the theorist must remember to take account of backward movements as well. A place must be found in the model for cyclical movements as well as for movement in a straight line. Indeed, it is likely that in pre-industrial societies, social change is usually cyclical. No wonder then that before the late eighteenth century people did not believe in progress but expected history to repeat itself. Nor should we assume that after the Industrial Revolution social change became exclusively linear and cumulative. It is to be hoped that a future model might specify the kinds of situation in which linear and cyclical change respectively take place.

The second point is about the causes of change. One explanation for the predominance of cyclical change in the pre-industrial world is their dependence on population movements which were themselves cyclical, for reasons explained by Malthus. A future model of social change should place more emphasis on demography than either Marx or Spencer do, but distinguish the situations in which this factor is either dominant or subordinate. Another conclusion which emerges from the case studies, more particularly from the last, is the inadequacy of a model of change which has no place for factors external to the society being investigated. There can be no return to diffusionism, but one might hope that a future model might deal with the 'fit' between internal and external factors, and discuss what makes some societies relatively open (or vulnerable) to outside influences, while other societies are better able to resist them – indeed, unable to do anything else. What is it that determines the assimilation or rejection of foreign invaders, foreign technology, foreign ideas (cf. Ottenberg, 1959; Schneider, 1959)?

The third point concerns the mechanics of social change, the importance of events and individuals, or, better, the 'fit' between events and individuals on one side and long-term trends on the other. In what circumstances and in what ways are social structures vulnerable to the impact of events? In what ways are they resilient? A number of historical studies suggest that wars and other crises often act as accelerators, speeding up social change rather than initiating it. Hence the same crisis can have opposite effects in different regions. In Britain, the 1914-18 War is said to have led to the 'blurring' of social distinctions; in Germany, to their sharpening (Marwick, 1965; Kocka, 1973). The war between Britain and France in the late seventeenth century also seems to have accentuated existing differences between the two states, making the French monarchy still more 'absolute' but reducing the power of the British king. Again, the price revolution of the sixteenth century encouraged the rise of the towns and the end of serfdom in Western Europe, but led to the decline of the towns and the reimposition of serfdom in Eastern Europe.

In what ways can individual decisions influence social development? It is as obvious that rulers cannot hold back social change as that Canute could not hold back the waves. Some rulers have tried. The Tokugawa regime in seventeenth-century Japan attempted to change the social structure by decree, declaring that the four main social groups should rank in the following order: samurai, peasants, craftsmen and merchants. The decree did not prevent wealthy merchants from achieving a status higher than many samurai. On the other hand, the abolition of the samurai by the Meiji regime after 1868 was a decree with important social consequences. Many ex-samurai went into business, a career previously closed to them. Still more important are the unintended consequences of decisions by rulers.

Again, the assimilation discussed a few paragraphs back should not be thought of as an automatic process. It is usually the result of a good deal of hard work. It may be useful to think in terms of the 'management' of social change. Where the Tokugawa regime failed to do this, the Meiji succeeded. In *The Leopard*, Lampedusa's penetrating novel of nineteenth-century Sicily, one aristocrat says to another: 'In order to keep everything as it is, we have to change everything.' Some aristocracies (notably the British) seem to have had a talent for changing in order not to change, for adapting themselves to new circumstances, for making sacrifices in the interests of survival. All these activities have their place in a model of social change.

However, one might hope that the model might also specify the kinds of situation in which this policy has a chance of success. Two independent but converging studies of aristocratic behaviour in nineteenth-century England and mid-twentieth-century Rajasthan may be cited here. Both studies emphasise the split in the ruling class between an upper group which was more sympathetic to change and a lower group which had more to lose. The lower group traditionally looked to the upper group for leadership. In this situation the group with most to lose by change was unable to organise resistance, the 'adaptation' policy of the aristocrats was successful and social change took place without violence (F. M. L. Thompson, 1963; Rudolph and Rudolph, 1968).

In short, historians may have a contribution to make to a future model of social change which would take more account of diversity and of long-term trends than previous models had done, and specify the alternative paths and the constraints more clearly than before. Such a model, which allowed for 'either . . . or . . . ', but also warned that 'if . . . then . . . ', would be of use to historians trying to understand particular societies as well as to sociologists in search of less inaccurate generalisations. Such a model should be eclectic in the sense of drawing on the most valuable elements in earlier theories, though not in the sense of including propositions which contradict one another. To move a step or two closer to such a model is a primary aim of this book.

Bibliography

Anderson, P. (1974a), *Passages from Antiquity to Feudalism* (London).
Anderson, P. (1974b), *Lineages of the Absolutist State* (London).
Ariès, P. (1960) *L'Enfant et la vie familiale sous l'ancien régime* (Paris), trans. as *Centuries of Childhood* (London, 1962).
Avineri, S. (1968) *Karl Marx on Colonialism* (New York).
Aylmer, G. (1961), *The King's Servants* (London).
Aylmer, G. (1973), *The State's Servants* (London).
Bailyn, B. (1960), *Education in the Forming of American Society* (Chapel Hill).
Barnes, J. A. (1954), *Politics in a Changing Society: A political History of the Fort Jameson Ngoni* (London).
Barth, F. (1959), *Political Leadership among the Swat Pathans* (London).
Becker, H. (1963), *Outsiders* (New York).
Bell, D. (1953), 'Crime as an American way of life', repr. in D. Bell, *The End of Ideology* (New York, 1960), pp. 127 – 50.
Bell, Q. (1961), 'Conformity and nonconformity in the fine arts', in *Culture and Social Character*, ed. S. M. Lipset and L. Lowenthal (New York), pp. 389 – 403.
Bellah, R. N. (1959), 'Durkheim and history', *American Sociological Review*, vol. 24, repr. in *Emile Durkheim*, ed. R. A. Nisbet (Englewood Cliffs, 1965), pp. 153 – 76.
Bendix, R. (1960), *Max Weber, an Intellectual Portrait* (New York).
Bendix, R. (1967), 'The comparative analysis of historical change', in *Social Theory and Economic Change*, ed. T. Burns and S. B. Saul (London), repr. in *Scholarship and Partisanship*, ed. R. Bendix and G. Roth, (Berkeley, 1971), pp. 207 – 24.
Bendix, R., and Lipset, S. M. (1953), 'Karl Marx's theory of social classes', in *Class, Status and Power*, ed. R. Bendix and S. M. Lipset (Glencoe), pp. 26 – 35.
Berger, P. (1963), *Invitation to Sociology* (New York).
Berkner, L. K. (1972), 'The stem family and the developmental cycle of the household', *American Historical Review*, vol. 76, pp. 398 – 418.
Bernstein, B. (1970), 'Social class, language and socialisation', in his *Class, Codes and Control*, vol. 1 (London), pp. 170 – 87.
Birnbaum, N. (1955), 'Monarchs and sociologists', in *Sociological Review*, vol. 3, repr. in his *Toward a Critical Sociology* (New York, 1971), pp. 57 – 80.
Bloch, M. (1923), *Les Rois thaumaturges* (Paris), trans. as *The Royal Touch* (London, 1973).
Bloch, M. (1928), 'Pour une histoire comparée des sociétés européennes',

Revue de synthèse historique, trans. as 'A contribution towards a comparative history of European Societies', in his *Land and Work in Mediaeval Europe* (London, 1967), pp. 44 – 76.

Bloch, M. (1939 – 40), *La Société féodale* (2 vols, Paris), trans. as *Feudal Society* (London, 1961).

Bois, G. (1976), *Crise du féodalisme* (Paris).

Bois, P. (1960), *Paysans de l'ouest* (Paris).

Boissevain, J. (1966), 'Patronage in Sicily', in *Man*, vol. 1, pp. 18 – 31.

Bossy, J. (1975), *The English Catholic Community 1570 – 1850* (London).

Bourdieu, P. (1972), *Esquisse d'une théorie de la pratique* (Paris), trans. as *Outlines of a Theory of Practice* (Cambridge, 1977).

Bourdieu, P., and Passeron, J. C. (1970), *La Réproduction sociale* (Paris), trans. as *Reproduction in Education, Society and Culture* (London and Beverly Hills, 1977).

Braudel, F. (1949), *La Méditerranée* (Paris), trans. as *The Mediterranean in the Age of Philip II* (2 vols, London, 1972 – 3).

Braudel, F. (1955), 'Histoire et sociologie', repr. in his *Ecrits sur l'Histoire* (Paris, 1969), pp. 97 – 121.

Braudel, F. (1958), 'Histoire et sciences sociales', *Annales ESC*, vol. 13, trans. as 'History and the social sciences', in *Economy and Society in Early Modern Europe*, ed. P. Burke (London, 1972), pp. 11 – 40.

Burke, P. (1972), *Culture and Society in Renaissance Italy* (London).

Burke, P. (1974), *Venice and Amsterdam* (London).

Burrow, J. (1966), *Evolution and Society* (Cambridge).

Cahnman, W., and Boskoff, A. (1964), *Sociology and History* (Glencoe).

Castiglione, B. (1528), *Il Cortegiano* (Venice), many English translations.

Chapin, F. S. (1935), *Contemporary American Institutions* (New York).

Clarke, D. L. (1968), *Analytical Archaeology* (London).

Cochran, T. C. (1953), *Railroad Leaders, 1845 – 1890* (Cambridge, Mass.).

Cohn, B. S. (1961), 'From Indian status to British contract', *Journal of Economic History*, vol. 21, pp. 613 – 28.

Cohn, B. S. (1962), 'An anthropologist among the historians', *South Atlantic Quarterly*, vol. 61, pp. 13 – 28.

Cohn, N. (1975), *Europe's Inner Demons* (London).

Collingwood, R. G. (1935), 'Human nature and human history', repr. in his *The Idea of History* (Oxford, 1946), pp. 205 – 31.

Collini, S. (1978), 'Sociology and idealism in Britain, 1880 – 1920', *European Journal of Sociology*, vol. 10, pp. 3 – 50.

Comte, A. (1864), *Cours de Philosophie Positive*, vol. 5 (Paris).

Couturier, M. (1969), *Recherches sur les structures sociales de Châteaudun* (Paris).

Dahrendorf, R. (1957), *Soziale Klassen und Klassenkonflikt in der industriellen Gesellschaft*, trans. as *Class and Class Conflict in Industrial Society* (London, 1959).

Daumard, A., and Furet, F. (1961), *Structures et relations sociales á Paris* (Paris).

Davis, N. Z. (1971), 'The Reasons of Misrule', *Past and Present*, no. 50, repr. in her *Society and Culture in Early Modern France* (London, 1975), pp. 97 – 123.

Dening, G. M. (1971 – 3), 'History as a social system', *Historical Studies*, vol. 15, pp. 673 – 85.

Dibble, V. K. (1960 – 1), 'The comparative study of social mobility', *Comparative Studies in Society and History*, vol. 3, pp. 315 – 9.

Dilthey, W. (1883), *Einleitung in die Geisteswissenschaften* (Leipzig).

Donajgrodzki, A. P. (1977), *Social Control in Nineteenth-Century Britain* (London).

Duby, G. (1968), 'The diffusion of cultural patterns in feudal society', *Past and Present*, no. 39, pp. 1 – 10.

Duby, G. (1978), *Les Trois Ordres* (Paris).

Durkheim, E. (1895), *Les Règles de la méthode sociologique* (Paris), trans. as *The Rules of Sociological Method* (New York, 1938).

Eisenstadt, S. N. (1963), *The Political Systems of Empires* (Glencoe).

Eisenstadt, S. N. (1973), *Tradition, Change and Modernity* (New York).

Elias, N. (1939), *Uber den Prozess der Zivilisation* (2 vols, Basle), trans. as *The Civilising Process*, forthcoming.

Elton, G. R. (1967), *The Practice of History* (London).

Erikson, K. T. (1970), 'Sociology and the historical perspective', *The American Sociologist*, vol. 5, pp. 331 – 8.

Evans-Pritchard, E. E. (1937), *Witchcraft Oracles and Magic among the Azande* (Oxford).

Febvre, L. (1942), *Le Problème de l'incroyance au 16e siècle* (Paris).

Foster, G. (1960), *Culture and Conquest* (Chicago).

Foucault, M. (1961), *Folie et déraison* (Paris), trans. as *Madness and Civilisation* (New York, 1965).

Frank, A. G. (1967), *Capitalism and Underdevelopment in Latin America* (New York).

Freyre, G. (1959), *Ordem e Progresso* (Rio), trans. as *Order and Progress* (New York, 1970).

Furetière, A. (1666), *Le Roman bourgeois*, in *Romanciers du 17e siècle*, ed. A. Adam (Paris, 1958), pp. 900 – 1104.

Gellner, E. (1958), 'Time and theory in social anthropology', repr. in E. Gellner, *Cause and Meaning in the Social Sciences* (London, 1973), pp. 88 – 106.

Gershenkron, A. (1951), 'Economic backwardness in historical perspective', repr. in A. Gershenkron, *Economic Backwardness in Historical Perspective* (Cambridge, Mass., 1962), pp. 5 – 30.

Gilbert, F. (1965), 'The professionalisation of history', in *History*, ed. J. Higham (Englewood Cliffs), pp. 320 – 39.

Gillis, J. (1971), *The Prussian Bureaucracy in Crisis, 1840 – 60* (Stanford).

Ginsberg, M. (1958), 'Social change', *British Journal of Sociology*, vol. 9, pp. 205 – 28.

Gluckman, M. (1955), *Custom and Conflict in Africa* (Oxford).

Goffman, E. (1958), *The Presentation of Self in Everyday Life* (New York).

Goldmann, L. (1955), *Le Dieu caché* (Paris), trans. as *The Hidden God* (London, 1964).

Goody, J. (1958), *The Developmental Cycle in Domestic Groups* (Cambridge).

Hay, D. (1975), 'Property, Authority and the Criminal Law', in *Albion's Fatal Tree*, ed. D. Hay *et al.* (London), pp. 17 – 63.

Heers, J. (1974), *Les Clans familiaux au moyen âge* (Paris), trans. as *Family Clans in the Middle Ages* (Amsterdam, 1977).

Hexter, J. (1955), 'A new framework for social history', repr. in his *Reappraisals in History* (London, 1961), pp. 14 – 25.

Hilton, R. H. (1976), *The Transition from Feudalism to Capitalism* (London).

Hintze, O. (1897), 'The individualist and the collectivist approach to history', in *The Historical Essays of Otto Hintze*, ed. F. Gilbert (New York, 1975), pp. 357 – 67.

Hintze, O. (1919), 'The commissary and his significance in general European history', in *The Historical Essays of Otto Hintze*, ed. F. Gilbert (New York, 1975), pp. 267 – 301.

Hobsbawm, E. J. (1971a), 'Class consciousness in history', in *Aspects of History and Class Consciousness*, ed. I. Mészáros (London), pp. 5 – 19.

Hobsbawm, E. J. (1971b), 'From social history to the history of society', *Daedalus*, Winter, pp. 20 – 43.

Hofstadter, R. (1968), 'History and sociology in the US', in *Sociology and History*, ed. S. M. Lipset and R. Hofstadter (New York), pp. 3 – 18.

Hopkins, K. (1978), *Conquerors and Slaves* (Cambridge).

Iggers, G. (1975), *New Directions in European Historiography* (Middletown, Conn.).

Jones, G. S. (1976), 'From historical sociology to theoretical history', *British Journal of Sociology*, vol. 27, pp. 295 – 305.

Kent, F. W. (1977), *Household and Lineage in Renaissance Florence* (Princeton).

Kocka, J. (1973), *Klassengesellschaft im Krieg* (Berlin).

Koenigsberger, H. G. (1974), review of Stone (1972), *Journal of Modern History*, vol. 46, pp. 99 – 106.

Kosminsky, E. A. (1935), *Studies in the Agrarian History of England*, trans. (Oxford, 1956).

Lander, J. (1969), *Conflict and Stability in Fifteenth-Century England* (London).

Lanternari, V. (1960), *Movimenti religiosi di libertà*, trans. as *The Religions of the Oppressed* (London, 1963).

Lanternari, V. (1966), 'Désintégration culturelle et processus d'acculturation', *Cahiers internationaux de sociologie*, vol. 41, pp. 117 – 32.

Laslett, P. (1968), 'History and the social sciences', *International Encyclopaedia of the Social Sciences*, ed. D. L. Sills (New York).

Laslett, P. (1972), *Household and Family in Past Time* (Cambridge).

Leach, E. (1954), *Political Systems of Highland Burma* (London).

Le Bras, G. (1955 – 6), *Etudes de sociologie religieuse* (2 vols, Paris).

Le Play, F. (1871), *L'Organisation de la famille* (Paris).

Le Roy Ladurie, E. (1966), *Les Paysans de Languedoc* (Paris), trans. as *The Peasants of Languedoc* (Urbana, 1974).

Le Roy Ladurie, E. (1972), 'The "event" and the "long term" in social history', in his *The Territory of the Historian* (Hassocks, 1979), pp. 111 – 31.

Lipset, S. M., and Bendix, R. (1959), *Social Mobility in Industrial Society* (Berkeley).

Lloyd, P. C. (1968), 'Conflict Theory and Yoruba Kingdoms', in *History and Social Anthropology*, ed. I. M. Lewis (London), pp. 25 – 58.

Lukes, S. (1973), *Emile Durkheim* (London).

Macfarlane, A. (1970), *Witchcraft in Tudor and Stuart England* (London).

Macfarlane, A. (1978), *The Origins of English Individualism* (Oxford).

McFarlane, K. B. (1943 – 5), 'Bastard feudalism', *Bulletin of the Institute of Historical Research*, vol. 20, pp. 161 – 80.

McNeill, W. H. (1964), *Europe's Steppe Frontier* (Chicago).

Maitland, F. W. (1897), *Domesday Book and Beyond* (London).

Malinowski, B. (1926), 'Myth in primitive psychology', repr. in his *Magic, Science and Religion* (New York, 1954), pp. 93 – 148.

Malinowski, B. (1946), *Dynamics of Culture Change* (New York).

Mannheim, K. (1936), *Ideology and Utopia* (London, 1936).

Mauss, M. (1925), *Essai sur le don* (Paris), trans. as *The Gift* (London, 1954).

Merton, R. (1948), 'Manifest and latent functions', repr. in his *Social Theory and Social Structure* (New York, 1968), pp. 19 – 82.

Merton, R. (1949), 'Social structure and anomie', ibid., pp. 121 – 60.

Mills, C. W. (1959), *The Sociological Imagination* (New York).

Momigliano, A. (1970), 'The ancient city', in his *Essays in Ancient and Modern Historiography* (Oxford, 1977), pp. 325 – 40.

Mommsen, W. J. (1974), *The Age of Bureaucracy: Perspectives on the Political Sociology of Max Weber* (Oxford).

Moore, B. (1966), *Social Origins of Dictatorship and Democracy* (Boston, Mass.).

Moses, J. A. (1975), *The Politics of Illusion: The Fischer Controversy in Modern German Historiography* (Santa Lucia).

Mousnier, R. (1964), 'Problèmes de méthode dans l'étude des structures sociales', repr. in his *La Plume, la faucille et le marteau* (Paris, 1970), pp. 12 – 26.

Mousnier, R. (1969), *Les Hiérarchies sociales* (Paris), trans. as *Social Hierarchies* (London, 1973).

Muchembled, R. (1978), *Culture populaire et culture des élites* (Paris).

Neale, J. E. (1948), 'The Elizabethan political scene', repr. in his *Essays in Elizabethan History* (London, 1958), pp. 59 – 84.

Neale, W.C. (1957), 'Reciprocity and redistribution in the Indian Village', in *Trade and Market in the Early Empires*, ed. K. Polanyi (New York), pp. 218 – 35.

Nipperdey, T. (1972), 'Verein als soziale Struktur in Deutschland', repr. in his *Gesellschaft, Kultur, Theorie* (Gottingen 1976), pp. 174 – 205.

Nisbet, R. A. (1969), *Social Change and History* (New York).

Ossowski, S. (1957), trans. as *Class Structure in the Social Consciousness* (London, 1963).

Ottenberg, S. (1959), 'Ibo receptivity to change', in *Continuity and Change in African Cultures*, ed. W. Bascom and M. J. Herskovits (Chicago), pp. 130 – 43.

Ozouf, M. (1976), *La Fête révolutionnaire* (Paris).

Parkin, F. (1971), *Class Inequality and Political Order* (London).

Parry, V. J. (1969), 'Elite elements in the Ottoman Empire', in *Governing Elites*, ed. R. Wilkinson (London, 1969), pp. 59 – 73.

Perkin, H. (1953 – 4), 'What is social history?' *Bulletin of the John Rylands Library*, vol. 36, pp. 56 – 74.

Phythian-Adams, C. (1972), 'Ceremony and the citizen', in *Crisis and Order in English Towns*, ed. P. Clark and P. Slack (London), pp. 57 – 80.

Ping-Ti, Ho (1958 – 9), 'Aspects of social mobility in China', *Comparative Studies in Society and History*, vol. 1, pp. 330 – 59.

Planhol, X. de (1972), 'Historical geography in France', in *Progress in Historical Geography*, ed. A. R. H. Baker (Newton Abbot), pp. 29 – 44.

Porshnev, B. (1948), *Nardodnie vosstanya vo Fransii pered Frondoi*, trans. as *Les Soulèvements populaires en France* (Paris, 1963).

Postan, M. M. (1972), *The Mediaeval Economy and Society* (London).

Ranum, O. (1963), *Richelieu and the Councillors of Louis XIII* (Oxford).

Roethlisberger, F. J., and Dickson, W. J. (1941), *Management and the Worker* (Cambridge, Mass.).

Rosenberg, H. (1958), *Bureaucracy, Aristocracy and Autocracy: The Prussian Experience, 1660 – 1815* (Cambridge, Mass.).

Rosenthal, J. (1967), 'The king's wicked advisers', *Political Science Quarterly*, vol. 82, pp. 595 – 618.

Rostow, W. W. (1960), *The Stages of Economic Growth* (Cambridge).

Roth, G. (1976), 'History and sociology in the work of Max Weber', *British Journal of Sociology*, vol. 27, pp. 306 – 16.

Rudolph, L. I., and Rudolph, S. H. (1968), 'The political modernisation of an Indian feudal order', *Journal of Social Issues*, vol. 4, pp. 93 – 126.

Rüter, A. J. C. (1956), 'Introduction', *International Review of Social History*, vol. 1, pp. 1 – 4.

Schneider, H. K. (1959), 'Pakot resistance to change', in *Continuity and Change in African Cultures*, ed. W. Bascom and M. J. Herskovits (Chicago), pp. 144 – 67.

Schochet, G. (1975), *Patriarchalism in Political Thought* (Oxford).

Shils, E., and Young, M. (1953), 'The meaning of the coronation', *Sociological Review*, vol. 1, no. 2, pp. 63 – 80.

Shorter, E. (1971), *The Historian and the Computer* (Toronto).

Simiand, F. (1903), 'Méthode historique et science sociale', *Revue de Synthèse Historique*, repr. *Annales ESC*, vol. 15, 1960, pp. 83 – 119.

Skidmore, T. (1964), 'Gilberto Freyre and the early Brazilian Republic', *Comparative Studies in Society and History*, vol. 2, pp. 490 – 505.

Spencer, H. (1904), *An Autobiography* (London).

Stone, L. (1966), 'Social mobility in England, 1500 – 1700', *Past and Present*, no. 33, pp. 16 – 55.

Stone, L. (1972), *The Causes of the English Revolution* (London).

Tentler, T. N. (1974), 'The summa for confessors as an instrument of social control', in *The Pursuit of Holiness*, ed. C. Trinkaus and H. Oberman (Leiden), pp. 103 – 26.

Thomas, K. V. (1971), *Religion and the Decline of Magic* (London).

Thompson, E. P. (1972), 'Rough music', *Annales ESC*, vol. 27, pp. 285 – 310.

Thompson, E. P. (1975), *Whigs and Hunters* (London).

Thompson, E. P. (1978), 'Class struggle without class', *Journal of Social History*, vol. 3, pp. 133 – 65.

Thompson, F. M. L. (1963), *English Landed Society in the Nineteenth Century* (London).

Thompson, P. (1975), *The Edwardians* (London).

Tilly, C. (1964), *The Vendée* (London).

Tilly, C. (1975), 'Reflections on the history of European state-making', in *The Formation of National States in Western Europe*, ed. C. Tilly (Princeton), pp. 3 – 83.

Turner, R. (1974), *Ethnomethodology* (Harmondsworth).

Veblen, T. (1899), *Theory of the Leisure Class* (New York).

Vinogradoff, P. (1892), *Villeinage in England* (Oxford).

Vovelle, M. (1973), *Piété baroque et déchristianisation en Provence au 18e siècle* (Paris).

Wallerstein, I. (1974), *The Modern World-System* (New York).

Weber, M. (1921), *Wirtschaft und Gesellschaft*, trans. as *Economy and Society* (3 vols., New York, 1968).

White, L. (1962), *Mediaeval Technology and Social Change* (London).

Williams, R. (1977), *Marxism and Literature* (London).

Wilson, B. R. (1966), *Religion in Secular Society* (London).

Windelband, W. (1894), *Geschichte und Naturwissenschaft* (Berlin).

Wootton, B. (1959), *Social Science and Social Pathology* (London).

Wrigley, E. A. (1972 – 3), 'The process of modernisation and the Industrial Revolution in England', *Journal of Interdisciplinary History*, vol. 3, pp. 225 – 59.

Index